CRITICAL ESSAYS ON

THE METAPHYSICAL POETS

Editors:
Linda Cookson
Bryan Loughrey

LONGMAN
LITERATURE
GUIDES

Longman Literature Guides

Editors: Linda Cookson and Bryan Loughrey

Titles in the series:

CONTENTS

PREFACE

Like all professional groups, literary critics have developed their own specialised language. This is not necessarily a bad thing. Sometimes complex concepts can only be described in a terminology far removed from everyday speech. Academic jargon, however, creates an unnecessary barrier between the critic and the intelligent but less practised reader.

This danger is particularly acute where scholarly books and articles are re-packaged for a student audience. Critical anthologies, for example, often contain extracts from longer studies originally written for specialists. Deprived of their original context, these passages can puzzle and at times mislead. The essays in this volume, however, are all specially commissioned, self-contained works, written with the needs of students firmly in mind.

This is not to say that the contributors — all experienced critics and teachers — have in any way attempted to simplify the complexity of the issues with which they deal. On the contrary, they explore the central problems of the text from a variety of critical perspectives, reaching conclusions which are challenging and at times mutually contradictory.

They try, however, to present their arguments in direct, accessible language and to work within the limitations of scope and length which students inevitably face. For this reason, essays are generally rather briefer than is the practice; they address quite specific topics; and, in line with examination requirements, they incorporate precise textual detail into the body of the discussion.

They offer, therefore, working examples of the kind of essay-writing skills which students themselves are expected to develop. Their diversity, however, should act as a reminder that in the field of literary studies there is no such thing as a 'model' answer. Good essays are the outcome of a creative engagement with literature, of sensitive, attentive reading and careful thought. We hope that those contained in this volume will encourage students to return to the most important starting point of all, the text itself, with renewed excitement and the determination to explore more fully their own critical responses.

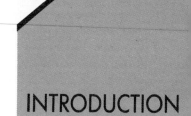

How to use this volume

Obviously enough, you should start by reading the text in question. The one assumption that all the contributors make is that you are already familiar with this. It would be helpful, of course, to have read further — perhaps other works by the same author or by influential contemporaries. But we don't assume that you have yet had the opportunity to do this and any references to historical background or to other works of literature are explained.

You should, perhaps, have a few things to hand. It is always a good idea to keep a copy of the text nearby when reading critical studies. You will almost certainly want to consult it when checking the context of quotations or pausing to consider the validity of the critic's interpretation. You should also try to have access to a good dictionary, and ideally a copy of a dictionary of literary terms as well. The contributors have tried to avoid jargon and to express themselves clearly and directly. But inevitably there will be occasional words or phrases with which you are unfamiliar. Finally, we would encourage you to make notes, summarising not just the argument of each essay but also your own responses to what you have read. So keep a pencil and notebook at the ready.

Suitably equipped, the best thing to do is simply begin with whichever topic most interests you. We have deliberately organised each volume so that the essays may be read in any order. One consequence of this is that, for the sake of clarity and self-containment, there is occasionally a degree of overlap between essays. But at least you are not forced to follow one — fairly arbitrary — reading sequence.

Each essay is followed by brief 'Afterthoughts', designed to highlight points of critical interest. But remember, these are only there to remind you that it is *your* responsibility to question what you read. The essays printed here are not a series of 'model' answers to be slavishly imitated and in no way should they be regarded as anything other than a guide or stimulus for your own thinking. We hope for a critically involved response: 'That was interesting. But if *I* were tackling the topic . . .!'

Read the essays in this spirit and you'll pick up many of the skills of critical composition in the process. We have, however, tried to provide more explicit advice in 'A practical guide to essay writing'. You may find this helpful, but do not imagine it offers any magic formulas. The quality of your essays ultimately depends on the quality of your engagement with literary texts. We hope this volume spurs you on to read these with greater understanding and to explore your responses in greater depth.

A note on the text

Wherever possible references are to *The Metaphysical Poets*, ed. Helen Gardner (Penguin, 1972).

Cedric Watts

Cedric Watts is Professor of English at Sussex University, and author of many scholarly publications.

ESSAY

The conceit of the conceit

When I mark students' essays on metaphysical poetry, I expect to find references to, and some definition of, the metaphysical 'conceit'. Frequently I'm offered Helen Gardner's excellent definition:

> A conceit is a comparison whose ingenuity is more striking than its justness, or, at least, is more immediately striking . . . It is used . . . to persuade, or it is used to define, or to prove a point . . . The poem has something to say which the conceit explicates or something to urge which the conceit helps forward.[1]

Next, by way of illustration, I'm usually offered the compass image in John Donne's 'A Valediction: Forbidding Mourning', in which the souls of the two lovers are compared with the points of a compass. At this stage, a mental yawn begins to spread between my ears. There are thousands of conceits in metaphysical poetry, and if the essayist cannot find an alternative to the example offered by Helen Gardner to illustrate her defini-

---

[1] Introduction to *The Metaphysical Poets* (Harmondsworth, 1957, revised 1972), pp. 19, 20.

tion, the essayist may be lazy or not bright enough to trust his or her own judgement. The argument proceeds, explaining how intelligent and apt the conceit is; and the essay may cite T S Eliot's early praise of Donne: 'A thought to Donne was an experience: it modified his sensibility.'[2] I may even be assured that metaphysical poetry thus exemplifies the 'un-dissociated sensibility', in which thought and emotion are splendidly fused.[3]

The common fault in such students' essays is that they say or imply that the metaphysical conceit is always *successful*. So, in response, I sometimes am tempted to argue that it always contains an element of failure. Even Helen Gardner's predominantly favourable definition contains its warning: 'a comparison whose ingenuity is more striking than its justness, or, at least, is more immediately striking'. Conceits are similes or metaphors; but what makes the reader say 'This is a conceit' rather than 'This is a simile' or 'This is a metaphor' is that a conceit is *odd* — *peculiar*; it draws attention to itself by its apparent incongruity or absurdity. Of course, in many cases we, after pausing and reflecting on it, see its logical or pseudo-logical justification. But what triggers our identification of it as a conceit is that moment of surprise or perplexity in which we think, 'This is odd; how do we make sense of this?' And in that moment, the flow of the poem is, even if only briefly, arrested. What may be a largely emotional response to the poetry is disrupted as we set our minds to work on the problem thus presented. Samuel Johnson long ago recognised that moment of tell-tale oddity when he said that in metaphysical poetry, 'the most heterogeneous ideas are yoked by violence together'.[4] Note the phrase 'by violence', which stresses the shock-tactics or effrontery of the conceit. *Chambers Dictionary* defines the conceit as 'a witty thought, esp. far-fetched, affected or over-ingenious'. It also offers a definition of 'conceit' of a less technical and more familiar kind: the kind we find in a conceited person: 'overween-

[2] T S Eliot: 'The Metaphysical Poets', in *T S Eliot: Selected Prose* (Harmondsworth, 1953), p. 117.

[3] See Eliot: 'The Metaphysical Poets', pp. 117–118. (This theory was later challenged by various critics, including Eliot himself.)

[4] Samuel Johnson, 'Cowley', in *The Lives of the Poets*, Volume I (London, 1952), p. 14.

ing self-esteem'. It seems to me that the metaphysical conceit can often convey a sense of 'conceit' in that latter, common-or-garden sense. The emphasis on mental gymnastics, on ostentatious cleverness, in typical metaphysical poetry can give the impression that the poet is an intellectually conceited person. A profusion of conceits may make the reader infer a conceited writer.

Helen Gardner's anthology, *The Metaphysical Poets*, appeared in Penguin paperbacks in 1957, and it has been reprinted numerous times. It's a fine anthology; again and again she has selected the best poetry in the metaphysical mode. It gives a very favourable picture. Nevertheless, I once saw a very different picture; and that was when I went to the British Library to look up Milton's 'Lycidas' in its original publication. 'Lycidas' is one of the finest elegies in the language: grave, sonorous, melancholy, indignant, plangent. The volume in which it first appeared was a memorial volume of verse commemorating Edward King, who had drowned in the Irish Sea. It was a double book, published in 1638: the first part (*Justa Edouardo King naufrago*) contains verse-tributes in Latin and Greek; the second part (*Obsequies to the memorie of Mr Edward King*) contains thirteen verse-tributes in English, Milton's appearing last. I found that almost all the English poems in the volume were in the metaphysical mode. Poet after poet seemed to be delighted by the prospect of ingenious comparisons opened by the fact that this young scholar had suffered an early death by shipwreck. Of course, the writers purported to be grief-stricken; but their profusion of clever conceits often gave an impression of almost callous ingenuity and of flattery meant to amuse rather than convince. Here's Henry King's reproach to the ocean:

> Thou sav'dst but little more in the whole ark,
> Then thou has swallow'd now in this small bark,
> As if it strove the last fire to outrunne,
> And antedate the worlds destruction.[5]

An anonymous contributor punningly declares:

---

[5] This and the subsequent few quotations are from *Obsequies to the memorie of Mr Edward King* (Cambridge, 1638).

> . . . we lament and weep
> Thy sad untimely fall, who by the deep
> Didst climbe to th'highest heav'ns: Where being crown'd
> A King, in after-times 'twill scarce be found,
> Whether (thy life and death being without taint)
> Thou wert Edward the Confessour, or the Saint.

John Cleveland's contribution begins with a wittily insincere declaration of sincerity:

> I like not tears in tune; nor will I prise
> His artificiall grief, that scannes his eyes:
> Mine weep down pious beads: but why should I
> Confine them to the Muses Rosarie?
> I am no Poet here; my penne's the spout
> Where the rain-water of my eyes run out
> In pitie of that name, whose fate we see
> Thus copi'd out in griefs Hydrographie.

Why, asks Cleveland, was King carried so prematurely to a watery death? Here's the answer:

> Some have affirm'd, that what on earth we find,
> The sea can parallel for shape and kind:
> Books, arts, and tongues were wanting; but in thee
> Neptune hath got an Universitie.

Thus, contributor after contributor enters the game of metaphysical wit and ingenuity, offering preposterous and ludicrous analogies: conceited parades of conceits. At the end of the book, however, comes Milton's majestic 'Lycidas'. Turning his back on contemporary fashion, Milton used the ancient mode of the pastoral elegy, referring to King by the classical pseudonyms 'Lycidas' or 'Lycid' (a procedure which gives the man legendary stature); the verse-form is expressively flexible; and tonally the work is strongly varied, but predominantly earnest and grave. There are even occasions when the floral prettinesses of the pastoral convention are dismissed as mere consolatory fancies which veil the harsh realities of death:

> Bid *Amaranthus* all his beauty shed,
> And Daffadillies fill their cups with tears,
> To strew the Laureat Herse where Lycid lies.

For so to interpose a little ease,
Let our frail thoughts dally with false surmise.
Ay me! Whilst thee the shores, and sounding Seas
Wash far away, where ere thy bones are hurld,
Whether beyond the stormy *Hebrides*,
Where thou perhaps under the whelming tide
Visitst the bottom of the monstrous world . . .

Thus, on reading 'Lycidas' in its original context, I gained a much stronger impression of Milton's power and originality. He was determined to offer an elegy which created the impression of troubled meditation on the moral and religious problems presented by the premature death of a fellow-poet; consequently, he was resisting the glib ingenuities of the highly fashionable and popular metaphysical mode. Those other tributes to King, by Cleveland and his kind, seemed by contrast to be exercises in superficial cleverness and excessive hyperbole. It's clear that metaphysical wit offers particular dangers when the poetic mode is one of elegiac tribute: the wit can resemble a heartless jocularity, and the customary praise of the dead person may seem a ludicrously fulsome sycophancy. These dangers are present in Donne's own poetry, though they become more evident in his imitators and followers. Even Milton, who usually pursued his own distinctive poetic course, was tempted in youth by the fashion, and the result was two weak poems on the death of Hobson the carter ('On the University Carrier' and 'Another on the Same'): 'His wain was his increase', remarks Milton, punning feebly on 'wain' (wane, wagon). Again, in the early works of John Dryden, who helped to establish the Augustan mode by writing verse with a new elegant lucidity and urbanity, we sometimes see the fatal attractions of metaphysical wit. Here's an extract from Dryden's elegy, 'Upon the Death of the Lord Hastings' (1649). Hastings, as you'll gather, died of smallpox:

Was there no milder way but the Small Pox,
The very filth'ness of *Pandora's* Box?
So many Spots, like *naeves*, our *Venus* soil?
One Jewel set off with so many a Foil?
Blisters with pride swell'd, which th'row's flesh did sprout
Like Rose-buds, stuck i'th'Lilly-skin about.
Each little Pimple had a Tear in it,

To wail the fault its rising did commit:
Who, Rebel-like, with their own Lord at strife,
Thus made an Insurrection 'gainst his Life.[6]

There you have a rapid flurry of conceits: seizing on the interesting fact that Hastings died of a disfiguring disease, Dryden's
wit gets to work. Those smallpox spots are 'naeves' (moles)
marring Venus-like beauty, or foils (metal settings) for a jewel;
the blisters sprang up because they were full of pride, and
resemble rosebuds stuck in lily-white skin; and as for the fluid
in each pimple, that was the tear for the pimple to shed in
remorse, because such disfigurements resembled rebels rising in
arms against their lord. Now, if I were a relative of young Lord
Hastings, I would not find such poetry consolatory; I might even
find it painful or disgusting. The poet seems to be expressing not
sorrow so much as glee at the opportunities for analogies; and
those analogies are deliberately hyperbolic or preposterous. It's
part of the fashion. The dominant characteristic of metaphysical
poetry — not the exceptional poems but the *representative* poems
— is the triumph of riddling ingenuity over common sense. All
too often, a poem in that mode resembles a sequence of rapid
riddles or even jests, regardless of the gravity or nobility of the
subject; and, since the effect of wit is often achieved by the
extraction of *some* sense from the most preposterous analogies
(or by the deduction of preposterous conclusions from plausible
premises), the effect is of dottiness: the mild craziness of writers
who are vying with each other in a display of deliberately
misapplied intelligence. Logic is simultaneously used and abused.

In fact, one of the most interesting critical questions is not
'Can you demonstrate the importance of the conceit in good
metaphysical poetry?' but rather 'How did the good metaphysical poets manage to contain and control the conceit?' When
John Donne is writing at his best, the strenuous rhythms, with
their deliberate irregularities, with their impetuous battering at
the constraints of the theoretical metre, often manage to create
the illusion of immediacy and spontaneity; we can readily imagine that we are listening to a strenuously and fervently

---

[6] *The Poems of John Dryden*, ed. John Sargeaunt (London, 1910), p. 176.

argumentative voice. Indeed, the grand paradox of Donne at his best is that, just as he exploits an extreme tension between the theoretical metre and the irregular rhythm of colloquial utterance, so he exploits a marked tension between intense feeling and almost neurotic mock-logic. It's the illusion of fervent immediacy and spontaneity which seems to sustain the whole. Look for consistent doctrine in Donne, and you'll be disappointed; sometimes he's a Platonic lover, sometimes he's a sensualist; sometimes he's an idealist, sometimes he's a cynic; now he's blasphemous or scurrilous, now he's pious. What gives identity and personality to his work is largely its effective mimicry of an argumentative voice: its particular tones, pacings, stumblings, emergences into eloquence after struggles with entanglements. It is not surprising that some of his most effective moments occur when the strenuous style coincides with a strenuous imagined activity, as in his Satyre 'Of Religion':

> On a huge hill,
> Cragged, and steep, Truth stands, and hee that will
> Reach her, about must, and about must goe;
> And what the hills suddennes resists, winne so

As the seeker after religious truth is imagined as a man struggling up a craggy hill, so the verse, in its syncopated stresses, obliges us to enact a struggle too. The effect is so persuasive that the metaphor of climbing, though detailed, becomes simply an effective metaphor rather than a conceit. If you like modern jazz, you should like Donne's rhythms, for, having established the basic metre (in this case the familiar iambic pentameter), he likes to challenge it with powerfully varied counter-rhythms. In that third line, for instance, the theoretical iambic metre is:

$$\smile \; — \smile— \; \smile \; —\smile— \; \smile \; —$$
Reach her, about must, and about must goe

but the practical colloquial metre, which we find after a moment of trial and error, is:

$$— \; \smile \smile — \; — \; \smile \smile\smile \; — \; —$$
Reach her, about must, and about must goe

Notice that the emergent rhythm clarifies the sense: 'about must ... about *must*' is not a duplication, for 'a*bout* must' means

'You have to progress *deviously and obliquely*', whereas 'and about *must*' means 'And what's more, you are *bound* to progress like that (because you're under a religious obligation to seek religious truth, if your damnation is to be averted)'. This poem, incidentally, is written in heroic couplets: the lines rhyme in pairs; yet when I ask students what the verse-form is, they often reply 'blank verse'. The reason for this erroneous response is that whereas, later, the Augustan poets were to make the rhyme-endings conspicuous (because their punctuation often marked the line-endings and thus induced pauses immediately after the rhyme), Donne preferred to dramatise spontaneity and struggle by using the rhymes as resistances to be overcome; repeatedly the enjambement seems to force the sense through the unavailing barrier provided by the rhyme, as in 'hee that will/ Reach her' in the passage quoted just now.

If we consider some of the most successful poems of George Herbert (for example, 'The Collar', 'Love', 'Dialogue', 'Affliction' and 'Redemption'), we find that though Herbert's temperament seems generally less pugnacious and combative than Donne's, the persuasiveness of the poems lies largely in their tonal control and flexibility, so that we can readily imagine the sounds of emotionally engaged conversation, dispute or dialogue. The dramatisation of feeling often succeeds in containing and curbing the tendency of the conceit to offer a distracting riddle; indeed, at his most sophisticated, Herbert offers arguments against argument and poems against poetry, sometimes criticising not only the traditional clichés of poetical convention but also the modish riddles of the conceited metaphysical mode:

> Shepherds are honest people; let them sing:
> Riddle who list, for me, and pull for Prime:
> I envie no mans nightingale or spring;
> Nor let them punish me with loss of rime,
>   Who plainly say, *My God, My King.*

('Jordan (I)')

Even here, one characteristic of metaphysical poetry is being maintained: the love of paradox.

That love of paradox, on both a large and a small scale, characterises the work of Andrew Marvell, whose range gives the impression that he is several different poets. Sometimes, like a minor metaphysical poet, he relishes quaint and dotty conceits; in 'Upon Appleton House', for instance, the local fishermen:

> ... like Antipodes in shoes,
> Have shod their heads in their canoes;
> How tortoise-like, but not so slow,
> These rational amphibii go![7]

At other times, as in satires like 'The Last Instructions to a Painter', he anticipates the Augustan urbanity (and deftly conspicuous couplets) of a mature Dryden or an Alexander Pope. Here he satirises the Countess of Castlemaine, a mistress of King Charles II:

> Paint *Castlemaine* in colours that will hold
> (Her, not her picture, for she now grows old):
> She through her lackey's drawers, as he ran,
> Discerned love's cause, and a new flame began
> . . .
> Poring within her glass she re-adjusts
> Her looks, and oft-tried beauty now distrusts;
> Fears lest he scorn a woman once assayed,
> And now first wished she e'er had been a maid.
> Great Love, how dost thou triumph and how reign,
> That to a groom couldst humble her disdain![8]

At his finest, though, in 'The Garden' and 'To His Coy Mistress', that Augustan poise in tone blends with, and controls, the mental shock-tactics of the conceit; and Marvell's distinctively sensuous, colourful imagining of location and situation converts what might have been merely quaint into the richly fantastic or surrealistic. Here, in 'The Garden', he offers benign transformations, firstly of the Ovidian legends in which deities sought to rape mortals, and secondly of the biblical account of the Fall of man:

> *Apollo* hunted *Daphne* so,
> Only that She might Laurel grow.

---

[7] *Andrew Marvell: The Complete Poems*, ed. E S Donno (Harmondsworth, 1972), p. 99.
[8] *Andrew Marvell: The Complete Poems*, p. 159.

And *Pan* did after *Syrinx* speed,
Not as a Nymph, but for a Reed.

What wond'rous Life in this I lead!
Ripe Apples drop about my head;
The Luscious Clusters of the Vine
Upon my Mouth do crush their Wine;
The Nectaren, and curious Peach,
Into my hands themselves do reach;
Stumbling on Melons, as I pass,
Insnar'd with Flow'rs, I fall on Grass.

There's a trace of the conceit in the first four lines, for Marvell, in order to support his hyperbolic praise of nature, offers the tongue-in-cheek claim that Apollo and Pan pursued Daphne and Syrinx not with intent to rape (as was the case — an intent frustrated by the females' metamorphoses) but in order that the metamorphoses of females into vegetation might occur. Then follows the paradox that in this present-day garden, a modern Adam without an Eve might still enjoy sensual bliss, might be wooed and won by delicious fruit, might be ensnared not by Satan as serpent but by flowers, and might fall not into sin and death but merely on to the carpet of green grass. Here Marvell moves beyond the realm of mere conceits into the realm of richly sensuous fantasy; he transmutes grim old myths into benign *new* myths to delight the hedonist. The metaphysical delight in paradox is preserved; but, after the arid mental gymnastics of an era of metaphysical conceits, that 'fall on Grass' accompanies a salutary fall into a sumptuously fecund imaginative realm. Marvell metamorphosed fanciful conceits into visionary fantasies.

AFTERTHOUGHTS

1

Need a 'declaration of sincerity' (page 12) be sincere?

2

How should one decide what constitutes a *'representative'* metaphysical poem (page 14)?

3

How does Watts distinguish between the 'merely quaint' and the 'richly fantastic or surrealistic' (page 17)?

4

What characterises the 'successful' use of conceits in the examples cited by Watts in this essay?

Graham Holderness

Graham Holderness is Head of the Drama Department at the Roehampton Institute, and has published numerous works of criticism.

ESSAY

Art and power: Marvell's 'Horatian Ode'

Marvell's 'An *Horatian* Ode upon *Cromwel's* Return from *Ireland*' (1650) has a number of distinguishing features, offering a range of different contexts in which the poem may be read. It is an exercise in classical form, harking back therefore to the earlier humanistic revival of Greek and Latin culture in the Renaissance: but its classicism is subservient to the exploration of a very modern theme. It is classical in content as well as form, since it continually compares historical events and characters of the present with those of the classical past. It appears to be only marginally 'metaphysical', since it proceeds by means of lucid statement rather than elaborate conceit; but such a 'plain style' (if it is in fact genuinely plain) would, in the art of the author of 'The Definition of Love', in itself be worth remarking. It has some clear relationships, in recurrent images and ideas, with some other of Marvell's most famous poems: but these relationships are often, as we will see, intriguingly contradictory rather than straightforward. Last of all, it is a poem deeply embedded in the history of its times: a poem about the Civil War, and about two of the great historical characters of that epic struggle, Oliver Cromwell and King Charles I. The Civil War was a conflict fought over grounds of religious and political differences.

Marvell's 'Horatian Ode' displays hardly any interest at all in religion. It is therefore, clearly and unmistakably, a political poem.

Poetry and politics

What is 'political poetry'? We normally think of poets and politicians as rather different types of people, with little in common, neither of whom would have much time for the other. How might the two activities be related? There are a number of possible definitions. In the broadest sense, a poem may be judged 'political' if it simply acknowledges politics as an important dimension of human life, and pays some attention to political matters, sufficient for us to say the poem has a political dimension. A political poem may be a poem directly about such political matters, yet still written from a point of view quite detached from the political process itself. Or a poem may be written to express or support a particular political viewpoint, to take one side or another in a political or party struggle.

It is at that latter point that most literary critics would begin to have reservations. They would assert that a politician writing or using poetry is likely to be doing so for his own party-political ends; and that a poet writing about politics from a position of party-political commitment is likely to betray the qualities normally considered necessary for the production of poetry — an open-minded and receptive sensitivity to experience, artistic and ideological freedom, and so on. Somewhere between the second and third types of poetry, in other words, we would normally expect poetic writing to cross the boundary between art and propaganda. Poetic writing that is clearly in the service of a political idea, subservient to a political ideology or even a party dogma, would generally be considered something other than genuine 'poetry'.

Marvell the republican

Where then does Marvell's 'Horatian Ode' fit into this critical problem? It is clearly a poem celebrating the actions of Cromwell. Though it may be more than fair in its treatment of Charles I, it is unmistakably, at least in terms of surface meaning, in favour of his execution. It could be described as a 'republican' poem, both in its spare classical temper and in its political ideology. In its obvious commitment to the Commonwealth, it is surely a 'party-political' poem, firmly positioned on one side of the political conflict.

None of this is in any way surprising, if we consider the basic known facts of Marvell's life. Little is known of his early biography, except that he spent a decade at the University of Cambridge, and travelled abroad in the early 1640s. Around 1650, when the 'Horatian Ode' was written, he entered the service of Lord Thomas Fairfax, who retired from his post as Commander-in-Chief of the Parliamentary Army in June of that year. In 1653 Marvell was recommended to a government post by no less a person than the great poet John Milton, and he joined Milton as Latin Secretary in 1657, after a period as tutor to one of Cromwell's wards. Marvell was elected MP for his birthplace Hull in 1659, and represented the constituency until his death in 1678. The poems written throughout this period are consistently republican and committed to the Commonwealth: in 'The Character of Holland' Marvell spoke of the Commonwealth as a providentially sanctioned state, the 'Darling of Heaven'; and his poem 'The First Anniversary of the Government under his Highness the Lord Protector' expresses uninhibited admiration for Cromwell as head of the republican state.

One would naturally expect critics to hold reservations about a poem, written by an obviously partisan individual, which celebrates the government of a particular political movement, and expresses adulation of the man who was supreme leader of both. And yet the 'Horatian Ode' has been consistently admired, even awarded the accolade of 'greatness', by critics who would certainly not have questioned the principle that poetry and political commitment are unlikely to mix. How did this anomaly come about?

Reading the Civil War

If we look at some of the formative critical readings of the poem, we will find that critics reconciled themselves to the poem by the simple expedient of transforming it into something other than a party-political statement. The 'Horatian Ode' is variously read as a disinterested account of Civil War politics, written from an uncommitted perspective; as a poem which grudgingly accepts Cromwell's authority, but expresses deep reservations about the nature of his power, and even covert sympathies for the Royalist cause; or a poem whose interest in the political dimension quite transcends the limited partisan perspectives of those involved in the ideological conflict of the time. In the words of F R Leavis, for example, the poem appears as 'the poised formal expression of statesman-like wisdom, surveying judicially the contemporary scene'.[1] In Leavis's reading, the poem's eulogy of Cromwell is quite impersonal (written with a 'cool appraising poise', p. 224). Its analysis of seventeenth-century politics is quite detached and impassive (a 'delicately ironic survey of contemporary history', p. 224). And its dramatisation of Charles I runs quite counter to any impression that Marvell may have been a 'party man' — the account of Charles's execution is, says Leavis, a 'deeply-moving evocation, sympathetic and sympathy-winning', a 'potent piece of propaganda' for the Royalist cause (p. 225). For J B Leishman, Marvell was a similarly 'disinterested' witness, writing 'without any profession of faith either in monarchy or republicanism'.[2] Leishman judges the 'Ode' a 'great poem', but only because Marvell was able to contemplate the phenomenon of Cromwellian power not from any position of political solidarity but with a fine aesthetic detachment. This critic clearly saw poetic and political activity as fundamentally incompatible:

> While one can say with complete certainty and without fear of contradiction that the world is the better for the possession of Marvell's poetry, it would perhaps be very difficult to maintain that it either was or is the better for his later political activities.
>
> (p. 20)

As this quotation testifies, in order to negotiate this difficult operation of splitting 'art' from 'politics' in Marvell's life and poetry, the critic tries to separate them in time and space. It was only 'later' that Marvell became engaged in 'political' activities (in fact of course the poem in question was written in 1650, right

---

[1] F R Leavis, 'Judgement and Analysis', in *A Selection from 'Scrutiny'*, vol. 1 (Cambridge, 1968), p. 225.

[2] J B Leishman, *The Art of Marvell's Poetry* (London, 1966), p. 13.

at the beginning of Marvell's active political career). Leishman takes this operation even further, by trying to infer, from very slight biographical data (such as the fact the Marvell had a brief flirtation with Roman Catholicism — at the age of 18!), and from the dubious evidence of some early poems, that in the earlier part of Marvell's life (about which virtually nothing is known) he was, in fact, if anything a Royalist. Helen Gardner in the anthology *The Metaphysical Poets* supplies a brief biographical sketch of Marvell which follows this line: 'The career and friendships of Marvell up to this time [1651], which it is thought most of his lyric poetry dates from, suggest that his sympathies were with moderate men, even with Royalists.'[3] 'Moderate' here is intended to suggest a position 'in the centre' of contemporary politics, a balanced neutrality that avoids 'extremes'. There is also the implication, however, that people who are in favour of retaining the status quo — even where that status quo may be a government as 'immoderate' as that of Charles I — are by definition more 'moderate' than those who wish to alter the established political situation. As we have seen, Marvell was certainly one of the latter, a committed republican.

The Falkland factor

In their approach to the poem, all these critics were in fact drawing on a very strong ideological tradition in British cultural criticism. The approach of this tradition is to look back at a conflict like the Civil War, which was by definition a historical moment when ideas and beliefs were so sharply divided that men were prepared to fight one another for them, and to value those individuals who in some way remained neutral, 'moderate men' who refused to join either party or to espouse either political 'extreme'. For example Matthew Arnold, a powerful influence on the formation of literary studies and literary criticism, wrote in the 1870s a brief essay on a man named Viscount Falkland, who was killed fighting for the Royalists at the Battle

---

[3] *The Metaphysical Poets*, ed. Helen Gardner (Harmondsworth, 1957, revised 1972), p. 316. Although Gardner's anthology prints poetry dating from the early parliamentary crises of the Stuart regime, through to the Restoration, her introduction does not so much as mention the Civil War.

of Newbury in 1643.[4] Despite the manner of his death, the distinguishing feature of Falkland's career is that he never finally reconciled himself to either side in the conflict: his views and his commitments continually crossed and re-crossed the partisan divides of Civil War politics and religion. We would perhaps expect this indecisiveness to make him in retrospect a ludicrous figure, or even a treacherous turncoat: but the *Dictionary of National Biography* holds him up as a martyr to 'moderation':

> If his memory is never forgotten in England, it is not for what he did, but for what he was. Throwing himself from side to side in party strife, his mind was at least too large permanently to accept mere party watchwords, and his heart was even greater than his mind.

> (p. 1160)

Falkland's inability to sustain a firm stand with either 'party' is here regarded as a kind of heroism. This biographical tribute undoubtedly owes much to Arnold's essay:

> [Falkland] was a martyr of lucidity of mind and largeness of temper, in a strife of imperfect intelligences and tempers illiberal . . . he and his friends, by their heroic and hopeless stand against the inadequate ideals dominant in their time, kept open their communications with the future.

> (pp. 593, 595)

Notice that last extraordinary phrase of Arnold's. It is another way of saying that the man was ahead of his time. But Arnold's way of putting it suggests that there in the middle of the Civil War was a fully formed late-nineteenth-century liberal, putting in bottles messages that would be received and understood over two hundred years later. The true heroism of the English Civil War is not, then, attributable either to those who fought for Parliament, or to those who defended the Crown: the titles of hero and martyr are due to those who kept aloof from the ideological divisions of their own time, and thereby prepared the

---

[4] Matthew Arnold, 'Falkland', in *Mixed Essays* (London, 1879). In *Matthew Arnold: Poetry and Prose*, ed. John Bryson (London, 1967).

way for that ideology of balanced neutrality we have already seen being applied to Marvell's 'Horatian Ode'.

What all the critics we have looked at want to find in Marvell is the kind of 'moderate' Matthew Arnold found in Falkland: someone whose mind was too large to be confined by contemporary ideas, and whose sympathies were too neutral to accept commitment to only one 'inadequate ideal'. What they want to find in the poem is evidence that Marvell did not really intend to express the wholehearted enthusiasm for a single cause that it appears to express; that a more detached and sceptical consciousness subverts the poem's propagandist simplicity. A reading of the poem informed by such a perspective would go something like the following.

Marvell the moderate

The poem opens with the expression of a preference for the arts of war over the 'inglorious arts of peace'. Marvell's poem 'The Garden', which seems a much more intimate and personal utterance than this public tribute to a great political leader, conveys exactly the opposite sentiment — 'How vainly men themselves amaze/ To win the Palm, the Oke, or Bayes' — so we could suspect that Marvell really valued the virtues of tranquillity and retirement more than political and military success.

Where the poem appears to be praising Cromwell, we can detect the possibility of irony: it is Cromwell, not the poet, who thinks the arts of peace 'inglorious', and whose 'restless' spirit can be satisfied only by incessant war. That unappeasable energy is prepared to attack the 'emulous' on his own side who dare to challenge his power, as well as the 'enemy' who oppose it.

Cromwell is compared to Caesar; but it was of course Caesar's declaration of himself as perpetual dictator that marked the end of the Roman Republic. The system of monarchy Cromwell has destroyed is described as 'the great Work of Time', brought by the Civil War to 'ruin' — as if Marvell regrets the wanton destruction of so venerable a political structure. The Royalist cause claimed 'Justice' and 'antient Rights' on its side: 'But those do hold or break/ As Men are strong or weak'. Here perhaps Marvell is subtly hinting at his sympathy with those 'antient Rights', and dissociating himself from the view that force guarantees justice.

It is perhaps the poem's presentation of King Charles that seems to provide the strongest evidence in this case:

> *He* nothing common did or mean
> Upon that memorable Scene:
> > But with his keener Eye
> > The Axes edge did try:
> Nor call'd the *Gods* with vulgar spight
> To vindicate his helpless Right,
> > But bow'd his comely Head,
> > Down as upon a Bed.

The tribute to Charles's impeccable behaviour on the scaffold can be read as a covert criticism of the man who had him executed. The comparison that follows brings this critical view to focus: the Roman 'Capitol' was, it is said, named from the discovery on its site of a severed head. The discovery was nonetheless declared by a soothsayer, observes Marvell with obvious irony, a good omen: 'And yet in that the *State*/ Foresaw it's happy Fate'. The poem then compares Cromwell to a bird of prey, to indicate the untamed savagery of his military policy (he has returned from a ruthless suppression of rebellion in Ireland, and is about to attack Scotland). The Commonwealth ('The Falckner') seems to control the predatory energy of the bird, but his control is tenuous. What if this massive and irresistible destructive power should escape from the control of the state?

The poem seems to end with a final irony, of particular significance to our 'moderate' critics: a state established on violence, whose founding symbol is the severed head of a decapitated king, can only survive by violence: 'The same *Arts* that did gain/ A *Pow'r* must it *maintain*'.

Marvell the revolutionary

It is clear that such a reading of the poem can easily be produced, and has a certain plausibility. But it is equally clear that in order to sustain this view of the poem, every detail of its poetic organisation, every image and phrase, has to be interpreted in the light of a single controlling assumption — that Marvell was the man of large mind, moderate temper and neutral sympathies, who seems largely an invention of the critics, and is curiously unlike the man we see emerging from Marvell's biography.

Let us, then, re-read the poem in the light of a different assumption: that Marvell's beliefs and sympathies were those one would expect in a man who returned from abroad in 1650 (perhaps after the execution of the King in 1649 made England a safer place) to form personal, professional and political connections with the great leading figures on the parliamentary side, and loyally to serve the Commonwealth under the Protectorship of Cromwell.

The opening of the poem certainly seems to allude to 'The Garden', and since the two poems express diametrically opposite attitudes towards retirement and public involvement, it would be natural for us to assume either that one poem negates the other, or that 'The Garden' can be used to detect irony in the 'Horatian Ode'. But seventeenth-century men were not so single-minded. They lived through a time when huge historical changes were effected through the conflict of opposing forces: ideas, religious beliefs, armies. Their thinking was often of that philosophical type we call 'dialectical': that is, aware of the co-existence of opposites, and recognising the clash of contraries as the dynamic of historical development. In common with other poets of the period, Marvell wrote several poems in 'dialogue' form — 'A Dialogue between the Resolved Soul, and Created Pleasure', 'A Dialogue between the Soul and Body'. The relation between 'The Garden' and 'Horatian Ode' is similarly dialectical: the desire for tranquillity and the impulse towards political action are both fundamental human needs, and their conflicting demands can be resolved only in the kind of conflict entailed in an open response to experience. Cromwell himself is presented in the poem as having encountered exactly such a conflict:

> Much to the Man is due.
> Who, from his private Gardens, where
> He liv'd reserved and austere,
>   As if his highest plot
>   To plant the Bergamot,

> Could by industrious Valour climbe
> To ruine the great Work of Time,
>> And cast the Kingdome old
>> Into another Mold.

It was no distaste for peace and retirement that drew Cromwell from his gardens, but the needs of history. Once that decision had been made and its consequences enacted, there could of course be no comparison between the comparative importance of raising plants and reconstructing a kingdom.

Another illuminating cross-reference could be made to another highly dialectical poem by Marvell, 'To His Coy Mistress.' It is often argued that that poem displays more sympathy with the fantasy of infinite time elaborated in the first section than it does with the *carpe diem* urgency of the last. Some readers recoil from the idea of love as a 'rough strife', and from the imagery of the 'am'rous birds of prey' devouring time before it devours them; and argue that Marvell's obvious preference was for the infinitely extended wooing described earlier in the poem. Such a reading of the poem is again dependent on the assumption that Marvell's instinctive sympathies were Royalist: since the endlessly protracted courtship is clearly a Cavalier idyll, and belongs to an ideology which assumes permanence and endless pleasure to be an eternally guaranteed prospect. The affirmation of urgency in the last section differs from the simple 'gather ye rosebuds' message of that same Cavalier poetry, since it is contextualised in a world of violent and disruptive historical change, where people are seizing their destiny and pushing history in new directions by sheer force of will — the world of the English Revolution. The energy and vitality which like an inward fire break through the woman's body in 'To His Coy Mistress':

> Now therefore, while the youthful hew
> Sits on thy skin like morning dew,
> And while thy willing Soul transpires
> At every pore with instant Fires

reappear in the 'Horatian Ode':

> And, like the three-fork'd Lightning, first
> Breaking the Clouds where it was nurst,

> Did thorough his own Side
> His fiery way divide.

Whether these formidable energies are directed towards love or revolution, they are surely in both cases being celebrated: but we need to read their urgency and their violence not in terms of quiet 'moderation', but in terms of the revolutionary forces shaping that new republican society in which Marvell played a leading role.

The 'sympathetic' presentation of Charles I could be explained again by reference to the dialectical character of Marvell's poetry: a commitment to Cromwell's cause does not prevent the poet from acknowledging the qualities of his mighty opponent. But we also need to take into account the manner of that presentation. Cromwell traps Charles in Carisbrooke Castle:

> That thence the *Royal Actor* born
> The *Tragick Scaffold* might adorn

If Charles was born to be an actor, to play a certain role in history (that of the royal martyr) it is only fitting that the new government should give him that opportunity, provide him with a stage. His performance is flawless, and could of course be read as an act of heroic martyrdom vindicating the Royalist cause. But a stage performance can by definition signify different things to different people: to the Republic Charles's unresistant passivity could represent an open submission to the people's authority:

> This was that memorable Hour
> Which first assur'd the forced Pow'r.

And the allusion to the founding of the Roman Capitol, far from subverting the claims of the English republican government, compares it with the great historical republic of Rome. We may recoil from the idea of a state founding itself in bloodshed, but Marvell was writing in a time of civil war, when such pacifistic inhibitions could have been regarded as inappropriate or even dangerous.

Lastly, the comparison of Cromwell to a bird of prey does not simply oppose innate savagery with external control. The

Falcon described in the poem exercises her own self-discipline: having once killed, she settles and searches no more, so that the Falconer's power over her is assured. The poem ascribes to Cromwell a similar self-discipline, suggesting that he has killed (i.e. subdued the Irish) for the state rather than for personal satisfaction or self-aggrandisement.

This reading of the poem has the virtue of some consistency with the historical character of its author — though that consistency may take the form, as we would expect in a 'metaphysical' poet, of dialectical ambivalence, paradoxical discontinuity between 'life' and 'art'. In order to reach such a reading it has been necessary to put aside the image of the sceptical, neutral, uncommitted poet who could look at his contemporary world from a position of transcendence; and from that point of vantage glance with a sympathetic eye across the centuries to our own ideological predispositions. In his place we have had to substitute the man who managed to combine 'poetry' with 'politics', artistic creativity with public commitment, literary achievement with unswerving dedication to a partisan position. If Marvell 'kept open communications with the future', it is by virtue of this willingness to speak poetically out of a deep immersion in the political currents of his age, and a loyal dedication to his party.

AFTERTHOUGHTS

1

How far should we rely on biographical information to determine our reading of any particular poem?

2

What do you see as 'the boundary between art and propaganda' (page 21)?

3

What differing interpretations of Marvell's presentation of Charles I does Holderness suggest (pages 27–30)?

4

Does this essay convince you that Marvell's 'Horatian Ode' is not the work of a 'sceptical, neutral, uncommitted poet' (page 31)? Compare Holderness's arguments with those of Gearin-Tosh (pages 89–96).

Ronald Draper

*Ronald Draper is Regius Professor of
Literature at the University of Aberdeen,
and the author of numerous scholarly
publications.*

ESSAY

The intellectual ingenuity of John Donne

T S Eliot did a great deal in the early twentieth century to
establish Donne as one of the most popular poets among academic readers. He found a unified sensibility in Donne which
had disappeared from post-seventeenth-century poetry, and
which he wished to see restored. Donne, in fact, became a stick
with which to beat Romantic and Victorian poets against whom
Eliot was in revolt. The *Songs and Sonets* became honorary
modernist texts.

However, as Rosemund Tuve and other historically and
linguistically based critics have pointed out, there is a great gulf
between the kind of poetry that Eliot writes and the kind
written by Donne. Although Eliot is correct in emphasising the
intellectual rigour which characterises Donne's poetry compared, for example, with that of Tennyson and Swinburne, it is
quite misleading to bracket that intellectual quality with the
allusive, argumentatively discontinuous method employed by
modernists, which makes their poetry 'intellectual' in a quite
different sense. Donne shares the colloquial immediacy and

B

freedom from metrical regularity which are two of the hallmarks of modernist verse (though it must be said that his metrical freedom is always related to a more traditional and more sharply defined base than is common with Eliot); but the technique of verbal collage — sudden, surprising juxtapositions of word and image without logically apparent connections between them — which is fundamental to the structure (or breakdown of structure) of much modern poetry, is completely alien to him. Greatly as he differs from those Elizabethan sonneteers and lyricists whose 'soft, melting phrases' are condemned by Carew in his 'Elegie upon the death of Dr John Donne', he is at one with them (and, it should be remembered, he began writing in the late Elizabethan period) in adhering to rational sequence and the normal syntactical forms of prose. He is likewise Elizabethan in his use of rhetoric, applying those figures of speech which were codified in countless 'arts of poetry' and formed the stylistic education of all literary men in the Renaissance. Spontaneity and verbal daring may seem to mark his poetry off from the conventional diction and decorative indulgences of his contemporaries and immediate predecessors, but the underlying methods and discursive procedures are the same. His commitment to reason is fundamental. The poetry is intellectual in the sense that it employs a linguistic mode suited to the needs of the conscious intelligence and is dedicated to the arts of argumentative persuasion.

This is not to say that Donne's poetry is didactic, or that his logic is watertight. Like Hamlet, he often prefers by indirections to find directions out. He frequently responds to the challenge of defending rationally indefensible positions, as in his prose *Paradoxes*, partly for the sake of recondite aspects of truth which may be discovered in the process, but mainly for the sheer exercise of ingenuity which is entailed. Many of the poems are entertainments, but imply a readership which is entertained by rhetorical and forensic display. An element of heterodoxy frequently heightens the effect: in the *Songs and Sonets* especially, traditional assumptions about love are often stood on their head with a typically youthful delight in being provocative. But the tactics matter more than the strategy. Invariably the means by which an end is achieved count for more than the end itself, which may be suspect, or even manifestly absurd. Yet the flexing of the intelligence in the process is a kind of end in itself and the expression of a vitality under admirable control.

A comparatively simple example is 'Womans constancy'. Its form is that of an imaginary debate between a lover and his potentially — indeed, predictably — unfaithful mistress, in which all the arguments adduced by the mistress in self-defence are anticipated by the lover. Laughable exaggeration is implicit in the poem from the start in the assumption that constancy can last no more than a day:

> Now thou hast lov'd me one whole day,
> To morrow when thou leav'st what wilt thou say?

And what follows is a tissue of arguments rapidly spun off, which amuse by their preposterousness rather than persuade by their cogency. Rhetoric and syntax cooperate to create momentary puzzles for the reader to disentangle, as in lines 8–10:

> Or, as true deaths, true maryages untie,
> So lovers contracts, images of those,
> Binde but till sleep, deaths image, them unloose?

In line 8 subject-verb-object (the sequence normally required in an uninflected language such as English to enable one to identify parts of speech) is disrupted to bring subject and object together, thus heightening the paradoxical parallelism of 'true maryages' with 'true deaths'. Then follows the dubious double analogy of 'lovers contracts' as images of 'true maryages', and of sleep as 'deaths image', which provides a vehicle for the argument that commitments made by lovers are ended when they sleep, just as marriages are dissolved when one, or both, of the partners dies. (There are also sexual overtones in 'sleep' and 'death' — a common trope for sexual intercourse — which add the cynical possibility that faithfulness can only be expected to last till the physical appetite has been satisfied.) The words 'true' and 'image' are also cleverly juxtaposed, and in the climactic argument constancy itself is made to consist of an equation between truth and falsehood:

> Or, your owne end to Justifie,
> For having purpos'd change and falsehood; you
> Can have no way but falsehood to be true?

In the last four lines any pretence that these are effective arguments is abandoned — they are called 'scapes' (= 'subterfuges'?), which the speaker declares that he could easily refute. However, his final coup of wit is that he deliberately chooses not to do this, 'For by to morrow I may thinke so too'. Thus 'Womans constancy' is a seemingly sexist poem on the banal theme that women are incapable of keeping faith, but one which shows in its end that the male speaker is even more unreliable. Manifestly, however, the poem's purpose is neither sexist nor antisexist; it simply offers an amusing collection of pseudo-rational arguments, followed by a neat dismissal of them to round off a clever forensic display.

In the Song, 'Goe, and catche a falling starre', the intellectual process is not so much forensic as studiously outrageous. An addressee is again implied, as in 'Womans constancy', and the 'thou' form assumes a degree of intimacy; but the interlocutor is now male rather than female. The theme is again the fickleness of woman — this time, however, set in the context of a young blade's affectation of cynical exaggeration.

In the first stanza, a series of commands to do the impossible is issued in somewhat flippant trochaics, and these are followed by two short lines which deliberately delay understanding of the purpose of the final command, so that when the reader gets there the cynical dismissal of honesty is effectively foregrounded:

> And finde
> What winde
> Serves to'advance an honest minde.

The second stanza employs more extended suspension as the anonymous 'thou' is urged to undertake a preposterously protracted journey, the duration of which is brilliantly conveyed in the fantastic image and crowded, stressed syllables of 'Till age snow white haires on thee'. Again the short lines dramatically hold up the final revelation, which is that no woman is likely to be found who is both 'true, *and* faire'. (My italics, but clearly required by the sense and the comma preceding 'and'.) Another 'if' clause opens the last stanza, conceding the possibility that this exceedingly rare combination might after all be found, but only to cancel it again as the speaker denies that there is any point in taking the trouble to meet such a paragon, since she will be 'False, ere I come, to two, or three'.

The attraction of such a poem is in its adroit control over the winding syntax, which mounts to a scoffing climax, or anticlimax, at the end of each stanza. Although there is no actual evidence of opposition, it is as if the speaker is engaged in debate with a conventional proponent of the perfection of woman (the 'thou' of the poem?), and is eager to discredit his views by debunking them. The arguments as such are slight, but the argumentative structure is skilfully managed; and the witty rhetoric at once amuses and dazzles, so that a momentary victory seems to be won.

A cynical gaiety is common to both of these poems, as is frequent enough elsewhere in the *Songs and Sonets* (for example, in 'Loves Usury', 'Communitie', 'Confined Love' and 'Loves Alchymie'); and the absence of emotional commitment is obvious enough as well. But in some of Donne's more intricate poems this is not so apparent. Even a manifest *jeu d'esprit* such as 'The Flea', where the speaker invents fantastic analogies between love-making and a flea-bite, is able to generate a degree of eagerness that gives the specious argumentation a touch of urgency beneath its display of wit. That the promiscuous flea, feeding on both the speaker's and his mistress's blood, can be apostrophised as their 'mariage bed, and mariage temple' carries imagination into the realm of absurdity; and it is, of course, instantly recognised as such. Likewise, the ingenious reasoning which turns the killing of a flea into the triple sin of murder, sacrilege and suicide is self-evident casuistry. But to treat the poem as merely an intellectual exercise (and I admit to having thought of it until quite recently in just those terms myself) is to ignore the sub-text of passionate wooing which makes these extravagances also capable of being read as the enthusiastic excesses of a sensually excited youth. Detachment and commitment are not so easily separated as one might think.

Still more is this true of poems like 'The Good-Morrow', 'The Canonization' and 'The Sunne Rising'. Here Donne can equally plausibly be interpreted as subjectively immersed in the torrent of love, or as mockingly exposing its topsy-turvy egocentricity. It is equally possible to regard him as involved in, or detached from, the experience; his arguments may be the result of reason being stood on its head, or poetic affirmations of the supremacy of emotion. They are teasingly difficult to read because they can be read in such contradictorily different ways; and yet they manage to convince even while the convictions they avow are transparently manufactured by the poet's freewheeling intelligence.

Such ambivalence is basic to 'The Sunne Rising'. Its opening — the celebrated mocking address to the sun, 'Busie old foole, unruly Sunne' — is a deliberate downgrading of the traditional aubade, or dawn-poem, and an inversion of the hierarchical associations of the sun with virtue, kingship, authority and power. 'Thou', in the second line, defies decorum, and the 'Sawcy pedantique wretch' of line 5 is cheekily intended to demote the sun from its assured place at the very apex of social and celestial dignity to the level of a pretentious upstart. Yet all this is simultaneously part of the colloquial intimacy which is fundamental to the warmth and youthful vigour of Donne's poetry; it is the chaff of boon companions, as well as the language of insult in a status-conscious society.

Similarly, the poem's satiric stance is ambivalent. As far as the speaker is concerned, the mockery is directed against time-serving worldliness. Sycophantic courtiers and place-seekers (ll.7–8) are contemptuously regarded as appropriate objects of the sun's attention (which is further degraded by being treated as a mere servant); and, still more daringly, the whole concept of worldly power is reduced to mimetic unreality compared with the high value placed on the love enjoyed by the speaker and his mistress:

> She'is all States, and all Princes, I,
>   Nothing else is.
> Princes doe but play us; compar'd to this,
> All honor's mimique; All wealth alchimie.

The zest with which this is proclaimed is its own justification; to make such large claims with such gusto is to communicate the intensity of the love-experience, and to set it in opposition to what the world takes for granted as its supremely important business: to inspire the reader with the same sense of disinterested aloofness from worldly considerations as the lovers themselves profess to feel. But at the same time the reader is humorously aware that such an attitude is anything but disinterested. The lovers are wrapped up in themselves, subordinating the entire external world to their own self-preoccupation. 'Nothing else is' is breathtaking, both in its glorification of love and its absurdity.

Donne, it may be said, has it both ways. He satirises worldlings, and simultaneously makes fun of his satirical spokesman, the besotted lover. Yet the poetry is still more ingenious than that. The speaker is carried away with his own ingenuity, addressing the sun, which he knows is necessarily indifferent to him, as if it were a personal acquaintance, and giving it preposterous instructions which are no more than would-be-logical extravagances extrapolated from the hyperboles used to express the lovers' relationship with each other. Since the mistress is all the world to her passionate admirer, and the sun's task is 'to warme the world', all it needs to do is to shine on the lovers. (Donne, who elsewhere reveals knowledge of the Copernican system, is here making use of the more poetically convenient Ptolemaic system which puts the earth rather than the sun at the centre of the universe — the lovers' bed thus becomes the planet which the sun is to revolve around, and the walls of their chamber its contracted orbit.)

A lover who actually believed that such an arrangement was possible would be madder than a modern flat-earther; but there is no need to suppose that in this poem Donne is inventing an insane spokesman, as Browning, for example, does in the dramatic persona of 'Porphyria's Lover'. The speaker's logic is merely at one with his poetic exaggeration. His hyperbolic claims for the supremacy of love become the premises on which his ingenious reasoning proceeds, and, carried to fantastic extremes, this is the result. The whole poem is essentially a magnificent extravaganza of the reasoning process, on a par with the delightful perversions of logic in 'The Flea', which deceives neither the speaker himself nor the listener. Its truth is the truth of fiction rather than the truth of fact.

Sir Philip Sidney, in *An Apology for Poetry*, is much concerned to defend poetry against the charge that it is 'the mother of lyes'. He argues earnestly that the poet offers his inventions *as* inventions, not seeking to deceive the reader into taking them for literal truth: 'Now, for the Poet, he nothing affirms, and therefore never lyeth' (*Elizabethan Critical Essays*, ed. G Gregory Smith, Oxford, 1904, vol. I, pp. 183–184). Shakespeare's Touchstone, in *As You Like It*, takes up the same topic, but treats it more lightly. He is concerned in particular with the 'lying' of love poetry, and deals with the accusation, not by refuting it, but by embracing it: 'the truest poetry is the most feigning, and lovers are given to poetry; and what they swear in poetry it may be said, as lovers, they do feign' (III.3.16–18). From this point of view, the more truly poetry functions *as* poetry, the more it departs from commonplace truthfulness. Donne would certainly agree with Sidney, but, in the *Songs and Sonets* at any rate, his spirit is more that of Touchstone: 'feigning' is the name of the game, and there is no need to worry about telling lies. He is also like Touchstone a master of chop-logic, and feels no constraint in using tricks of argument to bedazzle an opponent, or decorate emotion with plausible reasoning which does not constitute deception as such since only literal-minded readers would take it for anything other than feigning. The product, however, is not trivialised. The freedom from literal truth which is accorded by tacit consent to the poet, is a freedom to bring all the resources of language to bear on a given situation or theme in the interest of making it a more living kind of truth for the reader. Ordinary criteria do not apply; the poet is a law unto himself, a heretic in truth and logic, provided only that he captures the reader's imagination and succeeds in giving him delight.

Nonetheless, many readers would claim that some of the *Songs and Sonets* are more serious — or, to put it more cautiously, seem to be more directly committed to what they say — than others. There would seem, for example, to be a very considerable difference in the level of seriousness between 'The Flea' and 'A Valediction: forbidding mourning'. But if so, this is not simply a matter of the presence or absence of intellectual ingenuity. The latter is common to both poems. Its presence has already been demonstrated in 'The Flea'. In 'A Valediction' it is equally apparent in the 'conceit' of the compasses, where the idea of a spiritual union binding the lovers together, even when they are physically apart, is realised ingeniously, yet convincingly, in the image of a pair of compasses, the legs of which remain connected even though one is planted firmly at the centre and the other 'far doth rome' to describe the circumference of the circle. Admittedly, the three stanzas in which this idea is elaborated come at the very end of the poem, and it can be argued that Donne has carefully prepared the way for them earlier by creating an atmosphere of tender intimacy between the lover and his beloved.

The imaginative device which begins the poem is also an effective means of controlling tone and the reader's level of response. The hushed deathbed scene is yet another of Donne's typically dramatic opening gambits, but one that is in striking contrast to the flippant command at the beginning of 'The Flea' or the abrupt rudeness of address with which 'The Sunne Rising' opens. Here the imagined occasion is one which requires respectful attention and quiet sympathy:

> As virtuous men passe mildly'away,
> And whisper to their soules, to goe,
> Whilst some of their sad friends doe say,
> The breath goes now, and some say, no

We are present at the deaths of men who, being 'virtuous', have nothing to fear beyond the grave and therefore utter no anxious shrieks or groans. So quiet, indeed, is their passing that surrounding friends cannot tell precisely when their last breath is drawn. All is carefully muted and subdued. The choice of words and phrases such as 'passe mildly', 'whisper' and 'breath' (reinforced in the next stanza by 'melt' and 'make no noise') also helps to direct the reader's response. And the subsequent introduction of religious imagery in:

> 'Twere prophanation of our joyes
> To tell the layetie our love

further qualifies the occasion, enduing it with a sense of reverential awe.

Extravagances do exist in this poem, but they are used to throw into relief the less melodramatic, yet deeper and firmer quality of the love between the speaker and his beloved. Histrionic display and even genuinely terrifying events are made to seem insignificant by comparison with the quiet assurance of these lovers:

> Moving of th'earth brings harmes and feares,
>   Men reckon what it did and meant,
> But trepidation of the spheares,
>   Though greater farre, is innocent.

A contrast is also developed between the love of these now spiritually exalted lovers, for whom bodily separation is no disaster since they depend on the union of souls, and the love of 'Dull sublunary lovers' (existing on the merely earthly level, beneath the sphere of the moon, and hence subject to change and decay) which cannot survive without physical contact. Imposingly latinate polysyllables ('prophanation', 'trepidation', 'innocent', 'sublunary', 'Inter-assured') match this intellectual exaltation with a correspondingly rarefied choice of language, but the superiority claimed for mind over matter is perhaps even more effectively clinched in the plain monosyllables of line 20: 'Care lesse, eyes, lips, and hands to misse'. This, in its turn, leads into another conceit based ingeniously on the art of the goldsmith, which nevertheless gives the idea of spiritual union a vivid concreteness and immediacy:

> Our two soules therefore, which are one,
>   Though I must goe, endure not yet
> A breach, but an expansion,
>   Like gold to ayery thinnesse beate.

The atmosphere of serenity and the idea of spiritual union having been thus firmly established, the poem is now ready for its most daring extravagance:

> If they be two, they are two so
>   As stiffe twin compasses are two,
> Thy soule the fixt foot, makes no show
>   To move, but doth, if the'other doe.
>
> And though it in the center sit,
>   Yet when the other far doth rome,
> It leanes, and hearkens after it,
>   And growes erect, as it comes home.
>
> Such wilt thou be to mee, who must
>   Like th'other foot, obliquely runne;
> Thy firmnes makes my circle just,
>   And makes me end, where I begunne.

Separation and union are both allowed for in line 25. To be 'two' is to admit division, but to be 'two' in the manner thereafter explored by the compasses conceit is to accept that and at the same time overcome it. A pair of compasses (the very phrase is an interesting example of a joining of singular and plural) is a very precise, and very immediate, realisation of this paradox — 'stiffly twinned' to make one instrument, but composed of 'fixt foot' and wandering arm. Mutual dependence is also exactly expressed in the exercise of the instrument for the purpose of drawing a circle. It has sometimes been suggested that Donne's analogical thinking is flawed here, confusing the opening and closing of the compasses which bring the two points together again ('makes me end, where I begunne') and the fact that in drawing a circle the pencil will go right round the circumference, but come back to where it started. This, however, is conflation rather than confusion. The 'firmnes' of the 'fixt foot' (identified with the love and faithfulness of the beloved) in both instances acts as a control of the wandering arm (the lover) without which the perfection of the circle could not be achieved.

Intellectually, the analogy is satisfyingly appropriate. The compasses as a means of illustration is both surprising and exact. However, it is emotionally satisfying as well — because of the context which the preceding stanzas create for it (as I have tried to show), but also because the emotional values so important earlier are echoed here as well. Line 31, for example, 'It leanes, and hearkens after it', not only describes the action of tilting which accompanies the opening of the compasses, but conveys the feeling of yearning and eager, attentive concern of one partner for the other; and 'firmnes' in line 35 suggests both physical and emotional–spiritual stability — 'firmness', in fact, is felt throughout the conceit as a condition on which the relationship of the compasses and the lovers simultaneously depends.

The final rhetorical flourish that puts ending and beginning together is, again, literally applicable to the compasses' describing a circle, but, in addition, gives a sense of spiritual completeness. (There is an overtone of 'alpha' and 'omega', the first and last letters of the Greek alphabet which also stand for God, and possibly an echo of Mary Queen of Scots' last words: 'In my end is my beginning'.)

All this may be regarded as part of a counter-strategy to the one employed in 'The Sunne Rising'. In 'A Valediction: forbidding mourning' a subdued rather than violent opening builds up gradually to an elaborate conceit which impresses by its seriousness rather than its extravagance. The theme of the poem is under- rather than over-statement. Yet it is not a poem in which Donne rejects either intellectual ingenuity or rhetorical skill. That it seems more deeply committed (and may historically have been, if Izaak Walton, for example, is to be believed) is the result of Donne's adopting a different procedure for a different purpose, the clue to which is probably contained in the poem's title. A 'valediction' is a leavetaking, a 'saying farewell', in this case coupled with an attempt, not perhaps to banish grief as such, but to find comfort in the quality of a relationship which is too deep for noisy, irrational grieving. If I have referred to these lovers' love as having a specially profound, spiritual quality which is beyond that of ordinary sensual lovers, it is because the speaker is seeking to create just such a sense of what is valuable and worthy of admiration in the mind of the woman he is addressing. The 'teare-floods' and 'sigh-tempests' may already be in existence — or at least the speaker may fear that they are about to break out; and the purpose of the poem may be to calm or inhibit them. (In 'A Valediction: of Weeping' a strategy more akin to that of 'The Sunne Rising' seems to be employed, with a fancifully exaggerated creation of worlds out of tears in order to enhance the sense of the bitterness of parting and thus the intensity of the speaker's love; though in the last stanza the lover also pleads with the mistress not to be moon-like in creating a tide of tears which may swamp him — thereby, it could be argued, seeking the same goal of abating potentially excessive grief, but by a different route.) We are back, that is to say, with the poem as a vehicle of persuasion; and with Donne as a poet who may, or may not, be looking in his heart to write, but who is certainly consulting his art of rhetoric and choosing appropriate strategies.

My conclusion, however, is not quite that Donne can turn his hand to anything, while being committed to nothing. His virtuosity is such that he can (and on a number of occasions virtually does) argue that black is white and white is black. He can set up a super-seducer and equip him with dazzling casuistry, as in 'The Flea'; he can project an absurdly extravagant, though entirely sympathetic and condonable lover in 'The Sunne Rising'; and, going to the other end of the spectrum, he can create a spokesman who is a tender deprecator of emotional excess in 'A Valediction: forbidding mourning'. But he also does these very different things in ways that make it impossible, without damaging oversimplification, to compartmentalise them into entirely separate, unrelated performances. There are elements of adroitness and ingenuity in 'A Valediction: forbidding mourning', and of a passionate lover's zest in 'The Flea'. The complex personality of Donne informs his poems even when they seem to be detached from his own character and allowed to function as the ingeniously persuasive addresses of their imagined speakers.

Of Donne himself, a contemporary said that he was 'not dissolute, but very neat; a great visiter of Ladies, a great frequenter of Playes, a great writer of conceited Verses' (Sir Richard Baker, *Chronicles*, 1643, quoted in R C Bald, *John Donne, A Life*, Oxford, 1970). It is these features of the man which are revealed, though indirectly, in his poems, especially the *Songs and Sonets*, and which also give them their peculiarly paradoxical air of noncommittal, passionate commitment. They display the varied content of a flexibly vigorous mind, bold in its engagement with amorous experience of all kinds and brilliantly adept in taking a debater's role for or against almost any motion that might be proposed — a mind which delights in its own intellectual ingenuity and is capable of intense feeling, but which cannot easily be pinned down.

AFTERTHOUGHTS

1

Do you agree that the purpose of 'Womans constancy' is 'neither sexist nor anti-sexist' (page 36)?

2

What distinction does Draper draw between 'the truth of fiction' and 'the truth of fact' (page 39)?

3

Do you agree that 'Ordinary criteria do not apply' (page 40) in judging Donne's poetry?

4

Would you agree with Draper's summing up of Donne's 'mind' in the final paragraph of this essay (page 45)?

Michael Read

*Michael Read is Senior Lecturer in
English at Paddington College and an
experienced A-level examiner.*

ESSAY

Golden lamps and gilded clouds: Marvell, Vaughan and Nature

Marvell and Vaughan were born within a year of each other, and were writing the works upon which their reputations now rest at the same time: that, at first sight, seems to be all they have in common. Marvell was a Puritan, Vaughan a Royalist; Marvell was an active public figure, while Vaughan spent his entire adult life as a country gentleman and doctor in Breconshire. Turning to their poetry, the contrast is no less marked: Marvell is concise and technically fastidious; Vaughan diffuse and frequently clumsy in expression. However serious his theme, Marvell's writing is shot through with playful humour — not a quality one associates with Vaughan's work. Marvell, though by no means prolific, exhibits a very wide range of theme; Vaughan, even when compared with other exclusively religious writers like Herbert or Hopkins, seems to have an exceptionally narrow thematic range.

Why, then, bracket them together at all? Let us briefly consider Donne and Herbert. For Donne, a grassy bank is 'like a pillow on a bed'; he retreats to Twicknam Garden not to stumble on melons but to weep self-lacerating tears. Characteristically, he leaps from the intimate to the cosmic; transformed by sexual love, a little room becomes 'an everywhere'; America can be discovered in the mistress's body. In other words 'Nature' has no specially privileged place in his scheme of things. For Herbert, the spring is 'a box where sweets compacted lie'; a rose, however vividly presented, exists to teach a moral lesson. The sensuous 'attack' of 'The Flower' is at the service of a religious message: that all pleasurable experience is dependent upon spiritual health. Whereas Marvell rejects 'the Palm, the Oak, or Bayes' for the quietude of the Garden, Herbert in 'The Pearl' turns from learning, honour, and pleasure directly to God.

In this, Donne and Herbert are characteristic of their period. Even Shakespeare, alert as he is to natural detail puts this sensitivity to use as a metaphor illuminating human personality:

> Full many a glorious morning have I seen,
> Flatter the mountain-tops with sovereign eye,
> Kissing with golden face the meadows green;
> Gilding pale streams with heavenly alchemy

(Sonnet 33)

is a picture of the loved one, leading to the conclusion, 'Suns of the world may stain, when heaven's sun staineth'. My point, then, is that the interest that Marvell and Vaughan show in Nature as a thing in itself is worthy of note. Even here, though, a note of caution needs uttering. It is only since the late eighteenth century that the sense in which I am using the word 'Nature' — 'the countryside', 'plants and animals other than man' — has been current.[1] Neither poet, therefore, is working within a tradition of 'nature poetry'. If we look for the sensuous particularity of 'To bend with apples the moss'd cottage-trees' (Keats) or 'The leafless trees and every icy crag/ Tinkled like iron' (Wordsworth) we will be disappointed. We can, however, make this modest but significant claim: to Marvell and Vaughan, Nature offers experiences, or ways of coming to terms with experience, that can not be found elsewhere in the period.

---

[1] See Raymond Williams, *Keywords* (London, 1976) p. 188.

This is more obviously true of Vaughan. My opening paragraph suggested some reservations about his achievement, but one clearly successful poem is the uncharacteristically purposeful and concise 'The Retreate'. In it, the poet states his desire to return to a child's consciousness not simply for its innocence (even then a familiar idea) but for its visionary intensity:

> When on some *gilded Cloud*, or *flowre*
> My gazing soul would dwell an houre,
> And in those weaker glories spy
> Some shadows of eternity

A 'gilded cloud' is one with edges shining from the light of the sun concealed behind it. It is this image of light — specifically hidden light — that dominates Vaughan's poetry. For instance 'sinne/ Like Clouds ecclips'd my mind' ('Regeneration'):

> The Pious soul by night
> Is like a clouded starre, whose beames though said
>   To shed their light
>   Under some Cloud
>   Yet are above
>
> ('The Morning-watch')

> I search, and rack my soul to see
>   Those beams again
> But nothing but the snuff to me
>   Appeareth plain
>
> ('Silence, and stealth of dayes! 'tis now')

> The pursie Clouds disband, and scatter,
> All expect some sudden matter,
> Not one beam triumphs, but from far
>   That morning-star
>
> ('The Dawning')

> It glows and glitters in my cloudy brest
>   Like stars upon some gloomy grove,
> Or those faint beams in which this hill is drest,
>   After the Sun's remove.
>
> ('They are all gone into the world of light!')

I have quoted extensively (and could have found many more

examples) to demonstrate the variety of ways in which Vaughan uses this image. Its basic significance is so obvious it barely needs spelling out: light represents the state of ecstasy that the soul discovers in God; the clouds represent ignorance, the limitations existing within ourselves or imposed by the material world, hindering us from attaining this state. Had I been writing about Donne or Herbert, or, for that matter, Hopkins, I would have used the word 'relationship' rather than 'state'. This is an important clue to the kind of poetry Vaughan is writing. One cannot imagine him writing 'The Collar' or 'A Hymne to God the Father', because their effects depend on a sense of a personal God. To take a less familiar example, the following lines from Herbert are surely quite outside Vaughan's frame of reference:

> Who would know Sinne, let him repair
> Unto Mount Olivet; there shall he see
> A man so wrung with pains, that all his hair,
> His skinne, his garments bloudie be.

> ('The Agonie')

Someone else is always being addressed by Donne or Herbert — sometimes God, sometimes the reader; their poems are dramatic: Vaughan, we feel, is writing for himself; his poems are meditative or lyrical.

This essence, then, of Vaughan's best poems is the search for a spiritual state that cannot be achieved by means of a personal relationship, either with God or human beings. Nature is the medium through which this state is perceived and conveyed:

> O Joyes! Infinite sweetnes! with what flowres,
> And shoots of glory, my soul breakes, and buds!

> ('The Morning-watch')

What I find remarkable about these lines is their physical, almost sexual intensity. Vaughan is at once contemplating and experiencing the vitality of creation. I am reminded of a speeded-up film of a flower opening. A phrase like 'shoots of glory' illustrates Vaughan's distinctiveness in miniature. 'Shoots' are small, apparently mundane things, yet the reverse of trivial: they are charged with the 'glory' of growth and potential energy.

For a moment, Vaughan conveys not just what it is to be part of creation, but what it is to be a flower.

A few lines later he achieves a different, but equally impressive effect:

> In what Rings,
> And *Hymning Circulations* the quick world
>   Awakes and sings;
>   The rising winds,
>   And falling springs,
>   Birds, beasts, all things
> Adore him in their kinds.

The idea of creation as a harmonious whole is not an original one; what distinguishes Vaughan's vision is its sense of movement ('the *rising winds,/* And *falling* springs') and its three-dimensional quality. This is not a picture that Vaughan stands outside, but a picture of which he is a living part. The effect is achieved not through detailed description but through rhythm and diction suggesting activity. Consider particularly 'In what Rings/ And Hymning Circulations': as *description* this is vague, even obscure, but as a way of conveying a state of mind it is powerfully effective. 'Rings' suggests both the movement of the earth and the creatures on it; 'Hymning Circulations' adds birdsong and, implicitly, human voices joined in praise of God. 'Rings' and 'Circulations' together bring in the image of Eternity presented in 'The World'. Yet the very act of analysing such a cluster of images, of breaking it down, is like trying to grasp water; the images melt into each other like the forms of a baroque ceiling painting.

It is in the very essence of Vaughan's sensibility that such an ecstatic vision lasts only a moment. Elsewhere the very motion that so exhilarated him in 'The Morning-watch' is seen as debilitating; birds are 'watchful clocks', while:

> Man is the shuttle, to whose winding quest
>   And passage through these looms
> God order'd motion, but ordain'd no rest.

('Man')

In 'The World' the stillness of eternity is set against the futile bustle of human activity. Perhaps Vaughan's awareness that he is part of Nature explains the profound ambiguity of his feelings, nowhere better displayed than in 'They are all gone into the world of light!'

Whereas 'The Morning-watch' presents the material world itself as a 'world of light', here it has faded into 'Meer glimering and decays'. Vaughan's sense of a state of existence beyond this one 'tramples' on any pleasure to be found in day-to-day life. The frustration of *half*-seeing this world results in a call for release:

> Either disperse these mists, which blot and fill
>> My perspective (still) as they pass,
> Or else remove me hence unto that hill,
>> Where I shall need no glass

— if I cannot have clear vision on earth, let me die. The image of a perspective (telescope) obscured by mists encapsulates the contradictions within Vaughan's response to Nature. Is the created world something which magnifies and clarifies our image of God? Reading 'The Morning-watch', 'Cock-crowing' or 'The Water-fall' we might think so. Or is it a distraction that blots out true vision? 'The World', 'Peace' or 'They are all gone into the world of light!' provide equally strong evidence. Ultimately, I feel inclined to suggest that Nature is neither a telescope nor a mist, but a mirror. In a curious reversal of the notion of the artist holding a mirror up to Nature, Nature holds a mirror up to Vaughan, in which his own spiritual health is reflected.

Now consider these lines by Marvell:

> He hangs in shades the Orange bright,
> Like golden Lamps in a green Night.

('Bermudas')

There are many points of potential contrast with the passages quoted from Vaughan. Words like 'wit', 'playfulness' or 'specificity' come to mind, but above everything else I feel the lines are analytical and therefore open to analysis in a way that Vaughan's are not. Consider Marvell's use of the word 'shades': the shadows of the cool woods where the oranges grow, the dark leaves of the orange tree, and the shades of the lamps the oranges are compared to — all are clearly set out for the reader. This clarity of imagery directs us towards its significance. In 'Bermudas', just as in 'The Morning-watch', Nature presents an image of harmony and order. The difference is that while Vaughan sees heavenly order, therefore avoiding rational language that suggests human society, Marvell presents Nature as an ideal image of civilisation.

This is where, for the modern reader, Marvell's originality lies. We are more accustomed to poems that present Nature as offering values entirely different from, and usually superior to, those of society. This is because most poems of natural description we read are influenced by the Romantic movement whereas Marvell is writing within a pastoral tradition. I suspect all that many readers know of pastoral is a vague feeling that it has something to do with shepherds, so it seems worthwhile at this point to say a little about its history and significance. It seems to have originated with the third-century BC Greek poet Theocritus, although Virgil's *Eclogues* are the most influential classical example. Like other classical forms, it re-entered European writing with the Renaissance. The key elements are the presentation of an elaborately idealised version of the shepherd's life, frequently using as subject-matter either mourning a deceased fellow-shepherd or lamenting the unresponsiveness of a mistress (that is an idealised shepherdess). It should be immediately apparent that a contradiction exists in the very nature of the form: it is a sophisticated and artificial mode of writing in praise of a simpler way of life. Yet a moment's thought reveals a certain logic in the enterprise: only a relatively sophisticated society can look back nostalgically to a simpler mode of existence. And Marvell is a pre-eminently sophisticated poet.

The idea of 'looking back' is particularly important, and helps to explain why a classical and therefore pagan form retains its attraction to explicitly Christian writers like Marvell. One of the most important Christian myths is the notion of the Fall — the expulsion of Adam and Eve from Eden. This fits very neatly with the pastoral image of a lost Golden Age of innocence and untutored nobility. Even today, when it would be unrealistic to claim that we live in a Christian society, the notion of a golden age is a potent one in advertising and popular fiction (consider how frequently scenes are set in the recent, usually rural, past). Widespread and passionately held belief in declining standards in manners, respect for the law, architecture — one can name almost any field of human activity — testify to the strength of the pastoral myth.

The use to which Marvell puts it can be illustrated most simply by 'The Mower to the Glow-Worms'. The speaker is a mower (first cousin, as it were, to a shepherd) unhappily in love. The glow-worms are seen successively as reading-lights, comets, and torchbearers. These are not just arbitrary witty conceits, but essential to the pastoral notion of investing rustic images with 'civilised' properties. In the opening stanza the nightingale is presented as a poet; not the instinctive pouring forth of unpre-meditated art that a Romantic poet, such as Shelley (in his ode 'To a Skylark'), might have seen in her, but as a scholar, even a philosopher, studying, meditating and perfecting her art by the glow-worm's light. The wonderful second stanza effortlessly brings together the minute and the cosmic. Like comets, the glow-worms shine in the night; like comets, they have tails, like comets they portend the future. Indeed, they *are* comets: 'country comets', whose apparently humble role is to 'presage the Grasses fall'. 'Apparently humble', because the comparison invites us to consider which is more truly important; the fall of an individual however powerful, or the fall — literal this time — of the grass cut down by the mower, symbolising the seasonal cycle.

In the final two stanzas, Marvell moves to the poem's central idea. The 'officious' glow-worms (here simply 'helpful' rather than 'fussy', as the word would suggest today, but still a description loaded with the idea of an organised society) light the way of the travellers who might otherwise be led into the swamp by the will o' the wisp, but are of no use to the poem's speaker:

> Your courteous Lights in vain you wast,
> Since *Juliana* here is come,
> For She my Mind has so displac'd
> That I shall never find my home.

It is difficult to think of a word that carries more sense of the positive qualities of civilisation than 'courteous'. The life shared by the mower and the glow-worms is an organised and har-monious one. To describe someone as courteous implies equal good manners on the speaker's part. The entrance of Juliana shatters this harmony. At the start of this account I described the mower as unhappily in love: unhappily, but not necessarily unsuccessfully. It is not Juliana herself, but the complex and painful emotions stirred up by human passion that destroy the ordered rusticity of the mower's world, the one to which he can now never return.

Little T.C.'s world begins in 'simplicity', and ends with the threat of dissolution. Not so clearly a pastoral as 'The Mower to the Glow-worms', 'The Picture of little *T.C.* in a Prospect of Flowers' is clearly placed within the tradition by the description of T.C. as a 'Nimph'. T.C. as a child and figure from pastoral is doubly innocent. Like 'The Mower' it is essentially a nostalgic poem; this may seem an odd description of an anticipation of the adult life of a child of eight, but the scene depicted is one bound to pass away. Most of all, though, it is a poem about humanity and Nature. Little T.C. epitomises the power and fragility of childhood, a power and fragility *shared* by Nature. To us, of course, she is now inseparable from her prospect of flowers, yet the poem's force lies at least as much in emphasising an implied conflict. Whereas the Mower has, until the arrival of Juliana, lived in harmony with Nature, little T.C., though herself an innocent bud, is attempting to 'Reform the errours of the Spring'.

What are these errors? That tulips, for all their beauty, lack scent, that roses have thorns, that violets are so short-lived. T.C. is clearly a budding gardener (no trivial thing to Marvell). She is attempting to re-create Eden, just as, when an adult, her 'chaster laws' will try to rule 'wanton love'. But the mower has already shown us that innocence, once lost, can never be found again: however innocent T.C. is, she exists in an imperfect fallen world, a world that even Nature cannot provide an image of perfection for. Hence her quest is bound to fail, for Nature *does* provide an image of an imperfect world, where the thorns of roses stand for the pains and cruelties of love, the transience of violets the thin thread by which all our lives hang. It is this idea that lies behind the last stanza. It is as easy for Nature, at this moment 'courting' T.C., to nip her in the bud as it is for her to pick the buds of flowers she gathers — or to kill the hopes of the men who will court her. Adopting the role of the mower, Marvell laments the passing of harmony; speaking with his own voice, and writing about a real child, he faces it levelly and counsels acceptance of imperfection. Juliana will always come; to become an adult is to 'lose one's home'.

It should be clear by now that no simple formula will encapsulate either Marvell's or Vaughan's vision of Nature, but one generalisation may be helpful. Marvell and Vaughan both see Nature as occupying a space between human consciousness and God, a world of living things neither human nor heavenly. For Vaughan, the mystic, it can, at rare moments, provide a window to the heavenly world; to Marvell, the rational humanist, it presents an idealised image of what our lives in this world are essentially like. 'Idealised' but not expurgated: the roses in Marvell's gardens have thorns and the pastoral world encompasses pain and death. If Vaughan's poetry looks to Nature for answers, Marvell is content for it to provide the source for lucidly posed questions about the ambivalence of human experience.

AFTERTHOUGHTS

1

Do you agree with Read's conclusion that Nature, to Vaughan, is a 'mirror' (page 52)?

2

What do you understand Read to mean by 'analytical' (page 52)? Do you agree with this comment on Marvell's poetry?

3

Explain the relevance to Read's argument of his account of the pastoral tradition (pages 53–54).

4

Do you agree with Read's closing distinction between Vaughan and Marvell (page 56)? Do *you* see Marvell as a 'rational humanist'?

Charles Moseley

Charles Moseley teaches English at
Cambridge University and at the Leys
School, Cambridge. He is the author of
numerous critical studies.

ESSAY

'A sweetness ready penned': poetry, love and devotion in *The Temple*

Though some of the poems in it circulated in manuscript, Herbert never published *The Temple*. He left the decision to do so (or not) to Nicholas Ferrar: 'if he thinks it may turn to the advantage of any dejected soul, let it be made public; if not, let him burn it for I and it are the least of God's mercies'. But the book was immediately welcomed for the spiritual comfort and insight it could give its readers. Barnabas Oley, for example, pointed out the 'excellencies of Scripture, Divinitie, and choice passages of Scripture in metre'. Richard Crashaw, himself a distinguished poet, commented:

> Know you faire, on what you looke;
> Divinest love lies in this book:
> Expecting fire from your eyes,
> To kindle this his sacrifice.
> When your Hands untie these strings,
> Think you have an Angel by the wings.
>
> ('On Mr Herbert's Booke')

Among the discerning and the devout — who are neither necessarily the same nor necessarily not the same — it has never lacked readers since.

Yet Herbert's poetry presents contemporary readers with problems. In the first place, the Christian understanding of the universe and humanity's place in it is no longer something to be taken for granted of the vast majority of Herbert's modern readers; some, indeed, have not the slightest idea of the content of a faith that they casually reject yet which has formed the world they live in. Yet Christian religious poetry and art cannot be approached as if its central core of belief was simply an optional idiosyncrasy, with no more relation to truth than any other. Belief in a personal God and the possibility of a personal relationship to him is its very mainspring, and in religious art and poetry men and women are talking about the most important subject of all: their own nature, in all its brokenness, and its eternal destiny. To enjoy and appreciate the art of Herbert's poetry, it is not necessary to share his Christianity, any more than one has to believe in the Olympian gods to enjoy Virgil and appreciate his high seriousness. But it is impossible to do so unless one has an idea of the content of that faith, the Bible and the doctrines of the Church that centre round the saving grace of Christ, and a readiness to grasp the seriousness with which they might be, and often are, held. Conversely, to try to reduce Herbert's poetry to the level merely of a statement of religious orthodoxy is to miss utterly the passion, pain, ecstasy and struggle the poems record as his mind strove to understand its relationship to its Maker, its Lover, and its Redeemer and to express it in the intractable and slippery medium of words and poetic form.

Again, Herbert's is essentially private poetry, as intimate as the passionate intercourse between lovers, in which the words are merely the ripples on the surface that hint at what the water conceals. At best readers have the status of eavesdroppers on one half of an intimate, often passionate conversation. Herbert said to Ferrar that the book was 'a picture of the many spiritual Conflicts that have past betwixt God and my Soul, before I could subject mine to the will of Jesus my Master, in whose service I have now found perfect freedom'. Richard Baxter (1615–91), the Puritan divine who himself wrote a notable, detailed, spiritual autobiography, commented that Herbert 'speaks to God like one that really believeth in a God, and whose business in this world is most with God. Heart-work and Heaven-work make up his book.' Herbert is simply not interested in any other audience than the God whom he addresses so intimately and passionately — even as 'my dear' — and his art at its most complex and inventive, at the very frontier of what can be conveyed in words and form, is justified only by its devotion to a glory and a love which inevitably shows up its utter failure to capture the sounds of heaven in a net of words. The ultimate paradox is that the greater the artistry, the greater the perception of that artistry's inadequacy.

A book with an intended audience of one, so concerned with the intimacies of a relationship that goes beyond world and time, seems therefore to present formidable obstacles to its readers. Yet though it does help to share Herbert's faith — when the book becomes a delight that lasts a lifetime — even atheists, if they take the trouble to find out what Herbert was talking about, can be moved and exalted just as we all can be by the reading of love poetry — for example that of Catullus, or Petrarch, or Donne, or Sidney, or Spenser — which was not written to us: indeed, it may not have been written to any person at all but may simply be a clever game. For it is as love poetry (of, admittedly, a rather special sort) that many of Herbert's individual poems are best approached, and *The Temple* as a whole is a sort of Progress of Love from the first fumbling understanding and delight to the final acceptance and peace of union.

The title, *The Temple*, is richer in significance than might at first appear. Indeed, it might almost be said to alert a reader to the controlling double metaphor that unites all the poems in the book into a structure where each means more in context, and juxtaposed with its neighbours, than it can do on its own. In the first place, St Paul in 1 Corinthians 6: 19 and again in 2 Corinthians 6: 16, says that the Christian, and his body, are the temple of the Holy Ghost. This temple must be treated with reverence, and made pure and holy for the reception of the Spirit. Herbert's book, even in the unrevised form Herbert left it, is in considerable measure the record of the cleansing of that mystical temple. In the poem that opens it, 'The Church Porch', the emphasis is all on moral precept, on do's and don'ts — the outward appearance and behaviour of the soul seeking for union with God. But such prohibitions and injunctions are merely, so to speak, learning the alphabet. No code of morals worthy of the name is without such prudential advice, but its following, what Wordsworth called a 'cold abstinence from evil deeds', does little to transmute the mind conscious of its own sin into a soul on fire with a love so all-consuming that the prudent advice is no longer needed. And as we move on through the book, the interest more and more focuses on the development of an emotional and intellectual relationship, marred by dramatised backsliding and misunderstandings which have to be patiently understood, corrected, and purged, till in the last poem, 'Love (III)', 'Love bade me welcome: yet my soul drew back', the matured soul, still conscious of its own sin and unworthiness, is bidden to 'sit and eat' by Love himself. *The Temple* is thus the spiritual biography, so to speak, of the Temple of the Holy Spirit.

But there is another important idea to which the title alerts us. The Eucharist — the Greek word means 'giving thanks' — at which the soul is welcomed in 'Love (III)' is the central act of worship, at the altar at the far east end, in any real church building. We enter the book at 'The Church Porch', where, as it were, we wipe our moral shoes before opening the church door; it continues with a short verse entitled 'Superliminare' — 'Over the threshold' — and with it we enter a church building, when the first sight that greets our eyes from the west door is 'The Altar' and upon it 'The Sacrifice', an act of 'Thanksgiving' which unites the present moment to 'The Agonie' on Calvary — the next three poems, and the fifth. Though the scheme is not rigid, the book then takes us gradually down the aisle, seeing 'The Windows' on the way, looking at the marble of 'The Church-floore', passing 'The Church Monuments', hearing the 'Antiphons' and 'Church Musicke', joining in 'Prayer' and 'Praise', and seeing in all of them signs of the love of God and learning to read what they have to say. (Sometimes, Herbert's honesty reminds us, we get it wrong, or only partially right.) But as we move physically in this way, we are also moving through time in several ways: we move through the Christian life both in understanding and time. We begin with 'Holy Baptisme', we hear 'The

Call', undergo 'Discipline', attend at 'Mattens' and 'The Holy Communion'; we see the grey hairs, 'The Forerunners', that warn of our time running out, before facing at the end of the book the Last Things of 'Death', 'Dooms-day', 'Judgement', 'Heaven', and finally, being welcomed to the Lamb's High Feast in 'Love (III)'. Concurrently with this hinted-at physical movement which symbolises a moral and temporal one, is a cyclic movement through the Christian year: 'Good-Friday', 'Easter', 'Whitsunday', 'Trinitie Sunday', 'Christmas', 'Lent'. 'Lent' is followed by the longest section of poems of self-examination, praise and prayer in the book, before closing in the Four Last Things and, again, the everlasting Easter Feast. That movement through the year, a repeating cycle structured on the pillars of 'Sunday' and the liturgy — 'Mattens', 'Holy Communion', 'Even-song' — suggests again the process in time of the individual soul's learning and acceptance of redemption.

Such a complexity of symbol and structure, however loose it may be round the edges, argues that the poems are no mere transcript of emotional and intellectual experience as it happened. There is no doubt that behind many of them there is passion — indeed agony, as well as ecstasy; but these are extremities of feeling that have been transmuted by a mind recollecting them. When they do seem to be immediate, and the disorder of the form itself seems to capture the struggle of the soul, as in 'The Collar', we are aware of the disjunction between the 'I' of the poem and the poet: Herbert is standing aside from his own struggles in many poems, looking at the thrashing about of the will and mind with a calm and irony which depends on that struggle being now past and understood as part of the process of remaking — even if that remaking is not complete this side of the grave. Herbert's remark to Ferrar implicitly makes this clear: the manuscript was a 'picture', a transmutation into art, of the 'many struggles' of his soul, a turning of that which was, by definition, beyond words into words, a turning of fact into a fiction that records, as the love poem that is written after the event but as if in the heat of it records, the passion of love.

The paired sonnets, 'Love (I)' and 'Love (II)', make a clear distinction between the Love that, as Dante put it, 'moves the sun and other stars', which Herbert acknowledges as the 'author of this great frame', and the way the human mind in its fallenness, even when it knows this Love, ignores it and looks to other lesser loves for its joy. 'Mortal love', 'siding with invention', 'possesses heart and brain'. The theme of 'Love (I)', indeed, is the amount of wit and energy devoted to human love and love poetry while Love stands by, ignored despite the great gift of salvation given to men. The sonnet states the fact in some pain and resignation, yet offers no solution: he who should be the great theme of all art is rejected, and 'onely a skarf or glove/ Doth warm our hands, and make them write of love'. The sense of despairing failure is almost as plangent as in 'The Temper (I)', 'How should I praise thee, Lord':

> Lord! how should my rymes
> Gladly engrave thy love in steel,
> If what my soul doth feel sometimes,
> My soul might ever feel!

Herbert, like Donne in Holy Sonnet XIV, 'Batter my heart, three person'd God; for you', recognises that to know is not enough; without that grace of God acting on a man, that knowledge can never become the burning love that:

> Kindle[s] in our hearts such true desires,
> As may consume our lusts, and make thee way.
>
> ('Love (II)')

'Love (II)' is open prayer: a prayer for 'Immortall Heat' to refine the little fires that burn in men's minds and art, so that man's 'invention' — in poetry as elsewhere — may be laid on 'thine Altar', whence the smoke of its refining, like Abel's sacrifice, will rise to heaven in 'hymnes'. If God will grant this grace, then man's eyes shall see clearly: no longer the 'dust blown by wit' of this world and its art, which blinds the eyes, but 'thee'; he who legitimately claimed man's love but was 'disseized by usurping lust' — the legal imagery is significant — shall finally be acknowledged as Lord, and our 'eies' be 'mend[ed]'.

It is no accident that these two poems are sonnets, for though the sonnet form could do many jobs, it is particularly associated with the theoretical, highly sophisticated expression of emotion, particularly love. There is an obvious irony that two poems which clearly have as a major sub-theme the unease that Herbert has about art, including the writing of poetry, should be written in the most sophisticated form of all. This art directs itself to a partial rather than an absolute good, and through wit and invention can blind rather than clear the sight; paradoxically it is the more likely to do so the better it is. This unease surfaces again and again in *The Temple* — as if, like Marvell in 'The Coronet', Herbert recognises that even if a poem's genesis lies in the impulse to praise and glorify God, its writing can become self-justifying, an occasion for the pride and egotism of the poet to come between him and his subject — in other words, to take pride in his poetry and lose sight of its subject. As in Marvell, Herbert's finest devotional verse in its most elaborate art is inextricably bound up with 'wreaths of fame and interest' (hope of advantage or benefit). Near the end of *The Temple*, this issue is tackled head on. The last five poems all deal with events after death; the last earthly poem, so to speak, is 'A Wreath', a triumph of Herbert's art as well as its final rejection. It is a poem that, a *tour de force* of wit itself, undercuts all the sparkling artistry of the preceding poems, making us look at them, and itself, in a new way. The clever artistry of them all suddenly seems beside the point. We recall the 'friend's' advice in 'Jordan (II)':

> *There is in love a sweetnesse readie penn'd:*
> *Copie out onely that, and save expense.*

But that is what man, in his fallenness and need for God's grace, just cannot do.

'A Wreath', a mere twelve lines long, almost deserves a book to itself, such is its intricacy and complexity:

> A wreathed garland of deserved praise,
> Of praise deserved, unto thee I give,
> I give to thee, who knowest all my wayes,
> My crooked winding wayes, wherein I live,
> Wherein I die, not live: for life is straight,
> Straight as a line, and ever tends to thee,
> To thee, who art more farre above deceit,
> Then deceit seems above simplicitie.

Give me simplicitie, that I may live,
So live and like, that I may know, thy wayes,
Know them and practise them: then shall I give
For this poore wreath, give thee a crown of praise.

The poem is, literally, a wreath: it has a reversing rhyme scheme *ababcdcdbaba* where the rhyme words of the last four lines are the same, reversed, as those of the first four, thus returning in a circle to its beginning — and as George Puttenham said in 1589, a 'Round' or 'Circle' poem 'figures God in his infiniteness'. It is rhetorically organised so that the last idea of one line is the first of the next: the poem is literally woven, for the figure's Greek name is *Ploce* — 'weaving'. At the centre of the poem, always worth looking at in Renaissance poetry, which employed such spatial and mechanical symbolic structuring freely, is 'to thee/ To thee', while at each end is the action of the 'I' of the poem. The 'crooked winding wayes' of that 'I' are not only ironically and self-referentially represented in the construction and rhetorical organisation of the poem, but also twice opposed to God's ways: the first occasion is as far from the beginning of the poem as the second is from the end. The apparent humility of the poem is expressed in an extraordinarily complex and witty, intellectual pattern, and under it lurks a disconcerting pride: pride in art, pride that suggests the 'I' of the poem is doing and will do God a favour in giving him a 'wreathed garland' such as might be given to a victor, or a 'crown of praise' such as might be given to a king: who is 'I' to do this, and say patronisingly the praise is 'deserved'? The poem, the most complex structurally and rhetorically in *The Temple*, thus undercuts itself severely; but coming where it does, it also undercuts the artistry of everything that has preceded it. Herbert seems, in this poem, to be saying something like St Thomas Aquinas, who asked on his deathbed if he was not proud of his marvellous life's work in writing the greatest work of systematic theology in the Middle Ages, replied merely that it reminded him of straw: it would burn well.

So where is a solution? The sincere soul, seeking its progress towards union, is eternally trapped in its own fallenness. Even what Donne calls 'reason, your viceroy in me', which allows him to think and to write, is 'captived, and proves weak or untrue':

c

art seems to offer an escape but in the end reveals its own failure. The only way forward is the grace of God, a grace that accepts man in all his brokenness for what he is, and pardons it, and makes it the means of greater glory.

The three stanzas of the final poem, 'Love (III)', echo the triune deity of Father, Son and Holy Spirit. Here the soul is 'Guiltie of dust and sinne', and far from offering art and wit, draws back: it knows itself. The initiative is now Love's. Love accepts the bleared sight that prevents the soul from seeing clearly: 'Who made the eyes but I?' The soul, knowing itself, knows it has 'marr'd' its gift of sight and knowledge: Love 'bore the blame'. And finally, the soul accepts the welcome, accepts the forgiveness: 'so I did sit and eat'. The poem picks up and transfigures all those instances in the earlier poems where sight was dim, where dust blew off the 'Church-floore' and blinded the eyes, where the perishable dust was the subject of poetry rather than the imperishable love; and, for the first time, all the images of eating that run through *The Temple* like a leitmotif come together in the first act of eating in the book, for all the others were deferred. The Feast of the Mass, the Feast of the Lamb, the Feast of the Parables here coalesce in this final image of acceptance and calm that takes the poem beyond the stress of time and sin into eternity. All the asking for an impossible remaking is blown away in a realisation that God accepts us in our brokenness: 'Who made the eyes but I?' 'who bore the blame?'

Nicholas Ferrar's introduction to *The Temple* makes it clear that the book is not to be approached in any usual way: 'The dedication of this work having been made by the Authour to the Divine Maiestie onely, how should we now presume to interest any mortall man in the patronage of it? Much lesse we think it meet to seek the recommendation of the Muses, for that which himself was confident to have been inspired by a diviner breath then flows from Helicon.' Ferrar suggests that poetry that has been baptised in Jordan is qualitatively different from that which is watered by the Castalian spring, the sort of poetry that Herbert himself discussed in 'Jordan (I)' and 'Jordan (II)' and 'Love (I)' and 'Love (II)'. Yet this will not do: it almost suggests the poems are beyond normal criticism. As we have glimpsed in this short essay, they are not, and in fact the excellencies that normal criticism reveals put these poems near the top on any scale of poetic accomplishment. They are much more than just versified prayers, yet a progress of prayers they remain.

The acceptance we glimpse in 'Love (III)' was, in the end, extended by Herbert to his own creation, flawed and fallible as he shows it to be. But it is an acceptance which throws the initiative back onto the grace of God, to which finally he had made his will subject. On his deathbed his comment on *The Temple* was simple yet challenging, affirmative yet conditional: 'it is a good work if it is sprinkled with the blood of Christ'.

AFTERTHOUGHTS

1

Is it possible for someone who understands, but is hostile towards, the tenets of orthodox Christianity to appreciate Herbert's works?

2

Should the 'intended audience' of a book (page 60) influence how we read it?

3

Do you agree that *The Temple* should be approached 'as love poetry' (page 60)?

4

Has Moseley convinced you that Herbert's poems are 'much more than just versified prayers' (page 67)?

Peter Cairns

Peter Cairns is Head of English at Dean Close School, Cheltenham and an experienced A-level examiner.

ESSAY

The flint and the world of light: the originality of Henry Vaughan

The reputation of Vaughan's poetry has suffered consistently at the hands of critics and editors who assess him as an imitator or a poor version of another writer. 'If "metaphysical" means "Donne-like" Vaughan is an unimpressive metaphysical poet; if Vaughan is trying to emulate Herbert, he fails; if he is an exponent of his brother's[1] hermetic philosophy he is obscure and boring, and if he is an antecedent of Wordsworth, that is all he is.'

'Metaphysical', however, means more than Donne-like. The word refers in philosophy to the relationship between body and soul; in literary history to the characteristics of at least two generations of poets from 1590 to 1660: in particular to a delight

---

[1] Thomas Vaughan (1621–66), twin brother of Henry, wrote extensively on alchemy, 'natural magic' and mysticism, all of them aspects of 'hermetic philosophy'.

in drama and in the marriage of incongruous ideas and images, which often achieves a dramatic effect.

The themes of metaphysical poems are abstract. They may be the mixed feelings, the sweet sorrow, of lovers separating; the development of feeling from worldly impatience to religious acceptance, or, as often in Vaughan, the mixture of guilt and loss and hope after close contact with death.

As one might expect from the great age of English drama, the most private metaphysical lyric is dramatic in a surprising variety of ways. It often implies a little dramatic scene, a situation involving a dialogue, and changing attitudes in the characters. It usually contains argument which may persuade, or fail to persuade, at a dramatic climax or anticlimax. Like a play, it may present a variety of attitudes and a psychologically realistic complication of feeling. The poem may make a dramatic impact in other ways: by creating a sense of actuality and immediacy; by achieving effects of surprise in an explosive start or finish, or by confronting the reader with startlingly witty conceits. Most of these features are found in Donne: many are found in Herbert and Vaughan. Donne is always a more exciting poet than Vaughan, but the distinguishing qualities of the later poet are at least as precious as dramatic impact and dramatic intensity.

In the philosophical sense, Vaughan is more consistently metaphysical than Donne. Most of his poems describe or express a progress of the soul. Often his imagery gains an extra depth of meaning from its significance in the context of hermetic philosophy, the special study of his twin brother Thomas. This is by definition 'metaphysical', being concerned with mystic doctrine, supposedly derived from the Egyptian god Thoth, also called Hermes Trismegistus. It explores man's experience of God, and the relationships between natural and supernatural, mortality and infinity. This sounds obscure, and it can be when it takes us to the darker corners of alchemy, neo-Platonism and the Gnostic heresy. However, it is not, as some have suggested, a serious obstacle to the reader. Christopher Dixon goes some way towards a more measured response in an editorial introduction:

> He is in no conceivable sense a 'Hermetic' poet...He is a poet who uses the language and conception of the world of Hermeti-

cism because he found it a useful way of projecting his experiences, not because he wished to inculcate a belief in its somewhat extraordinary and highly complex tenets, nor even because he believed them himself.

(A Selection from Henry Vaughan, ed. Christopher Dixon
Harlow, 1967)

However, this source of imagery presents even less of a problem than Dixon suggests. Hermeticism is, like poetry, based on relationships and analogies. Its terminology usually has the immediate force of accepted metaphor. Words like 'influence', 'hatch', 'seed', 'beam', 'glance' and 'ray', which have a precise philosophical significance in Thomas Vaughan's 'Aula Lucis' or 'House of Light' (1652), mean what you think they mean in his brother's poems more often than not. So, when Dixon says of 'Cock-crowing': 'This is perhaps Vaughan's most difficult poem . . . in its wide range of allusions to Hermetic themes and Biblical symbols and in its technical Hermetic vocabulary', he conveys a false impression. The poem is not difficult and the Hermetic diction and ideas in no way obscure or confuse the reader's response to the charm of the analogy or to the fervency of the prayer.

> Their eyes watch for the morning hue,
> Their little grain expelling night
> So shines and sings, as if it knew
> The path unto the house of light.
>> It seems their candle, howe'r done,
>> Was tinn'd and lighted at the sunne.
>
> If such a tincture, such a touch,
> So firm a longing can impowre
> Shall thy own image think it much
> To watch for thy appearing hour?
>> If a meer blast so fill the sail,
>> Shall not the breath of God prevail?

The cock is painted in a stylised emblematic mode, but the picture is vivid and appealing, and the religious theme of sadness and guilt that man's soul fails to respond to the beauty of the universe is clearly expressed. It is not much enhanced by reading in Thomas Vaughan that the soul . . . 'is guided in her

Operations by a Spiritual Metaphysical graine, a seede or glance of Light . . .'[2] The simple diction which describes the emblem has the same force and appeal as the child's language in Blake. In some respects it is the same kind of imaginative world: dreamlike, visual, natural, unexpected, symbolic; and the pre-occupations are philosophical in the same way: images represent sound, sick or sinful attitudes of mind which an innocent child may have had or been immune from.

For the Romantics, Vaughan was good when he was like Wordsworth, anticipating the 'Immortality' ode by 150 years. Even as recently as 1987, Professor Vickers, writing of 'Jonson, Herbert and the Emblem', states 'Vaughan's individual voice emerges most strongly in the poems dealing with childhood'. Vickers misses the centre by a long way; and the rest of his summary is typical of much of the treatment Vaughan receives:

> Vaughan wrote few wholly successful poems, although he is capable of striking openings . . . and can at times sustain a complex argument. Yet too often inspiration vanishes
>
> *Oxford Illustrated History of English Literature*, ed. P Rogers
> (Oxford, 1987), Chap. 4.

Helen Gardner's anthology, which has most of the very best of Vaughan, contains only one poem about childhood, yet even she encourages negative attitudes to him when she writes in her Introduction:

> The fading of this desire to make poems out of particular moments, made imaginatively present rather than remembered, and played over by wit rather than reflected upon, is apparent towards the end of this volume.
>
> (*The Metaphysical Poets*, p. 24)

Vaughan is indeed more reflective than Donne, but he is as dramatic as Herbert, though in different ways, and more 'actual' in the sense that Gardner describes here.

Vaughan, although not often Donne-like is metaphysical; although inspired so much by Herbert that he frequently imi-

---

[2] *Anima Magica Absondita or a Discourse on the Universal Spirit of Nature* (1650)

tates him is very different; although interested in his brother's philosophy is not a philosopher, and although at the end of the metaphysical period is a new and moving voice, is not a decadent. Helen Gardner is much more helpful when she writes, 'The metaphysical style heightens and liberates personality. It is essentially a style in which individuality is expressed.' Critics are therefore insensitive when they judge one metaphysical poet against another in an attempt to present the whole group under one heading.

There are many ways in which Vaughan speaks for his age, and this is not the age of Donne or Herbert. Before he was thirty he had seen his public, religious and domestic world destroyed: his king, his Church, his wife, younger brother and several close friends had all died in the space of two to three years. Small wonder that the religion which now consoled him was a very private business; that the past seemed like a paradise lost; that he felt he was punished for some profound guilt, or that he took refuge in a remote rural scene.[3]

The individuality of Henry Vaughan, the quality which makes him such a remarkable figure in seventeenth-century poetry, is symbolised in the emblematic frontispiece to his first great poetic publication called *Silex Scintillans*.[4] There is a picture of the right hand of God striking a flame from a heart-shaped block of flint. Beneath it is the blazon 'Silex Scintillans or Sacred Poems and Private Ejaculations by Henry Vaughan, Silurist'.[5]

This is what his best poetry is. Here are suggested the contrasts between the Valley of the Shadow of Death and the World of Light, and all the paradoxical interplay of darkness and radiancy. Here also we are reminded of the fusion of the emblematic and the actual: the Hermetic symbol of the academic

---

[3] Perhaps there is an interesting irony that Marvell, the Protector's Latin Secretary, found haven in the elaborate gardens of Nun Appleton House, while Vaughan, a Laudian Churchman, sought solace in the wilds of Wales.

[4] *Silex Scintillans*: literally, the sparkling flint; usually translated 'Sparks from the Flint'.

[5] Silurist: Brecon, Vaughan's native town, was inhabited in ancient times by the British tribe of Silures.

and the immediate responses of a 'Silurist' poet, proud of his Welsh hills.

The black flint represents the poet's hard heart, but also the dark night of suffering and grief which made him so conscious of sin. This is felt most movingly in the nine poems without titles marked by a paragraph symbol in the editions of 1650 and 1655. Most of them refer directly to a recent death, either of his brother William, or of his wife Catherine. These poems are so movingly tender, disturbingly personal, so effectively structured and metrically varied, it is difficult to understand how the *Cambridge Illustrated History of Literature* can refer to verse movements being stiff and jerky, 'inspiration vanishing and long and short lines unanimated by any inner rhythm'. From the shortest of them, 'Joy of my life' and 'Come, come, what doe I here?', through the more complex 'Silence, and stealth of dayes! 'tis now' and 'Thou that knowest for whom I mourn' to the extended meditation 'I walkt the other day (to spend my hour)' and the masterpiece 'They are all gone into the world of light!', there is a consistent poetic power and depth of feeling at least the equal of, say, Donne's 'Nocturnall upon S. Lucies day'. Donne is writing as a lover striving to *describe* a sense of unique and absolute desolation after the death of his beloved: Vaughan is writing as a brother and husband trying to live on after the loss of brother or wife and to *express* that complex mixture of feelings which we all have to cope with sooner or later: loss, guilt, love, yearning, incomprehension and a desperate need to have something to hope for.

Notice the various dramatic qualities of those opening lines: the imaginative impact of 'They' and 'the world of light'; the quiet mystery of 'Silence, and stealth of dayes'; the surprising casualness of 'I walkt the other day'; the simplicity and immediacy of the pronouns and the direct address in 'Come, come' and 'Thou that knowest'. As perhaps with Donne, but hardly at all with Herbert, this is an actual situation. It involves the poet and a real death. It is very private poetry:

> Silence, and stealth of dayes! 'tis now
>   Since thou art gone,
> Twelve hundred houres, and not a brow
>   But Clouds hang on.

How imperceptibly and irretrievably a life slips away into the nothingness of the past, and how poignantly Vaughan presents that instinct which takes us back to the last moment of life a second before there is nothing but an empty husk:

> As he that in some Caves thick damp
>   Lockt from the light,
> Fixeth a solitary lamp,
>   To brave the night
> And walking from his Sun, when past
>   That glim'ring Ray
> Cuts through the heavy mists in haste
>   Back to his day,
> So o'r fled minutes I retreat
>   Unto that hour
> Which shew'd thee last, but did defeat
>   Thy light, and pow'r,
> I search, and rack my soul to see
>   Those beams again
> But nothing but the snuff to me
>   Appeareth plain

Here emotion is both described and expressed in equal measure. Desolation is not an abstract thing described and defined intellectually in isolation as in the 'Nocturnall'. It is the memory of a dead face and the loneliness of being lost in a fog at night, perhaps on a Welsh hillside. If these lines make an emotional impact it has little to do with Plato's cave and the reflected light of God, but it owes much to imagery from personal experience, strikingly simple diction and the tentative stumbling rhythms of searching. The search is an abstract image which is intellectually appropriate, but what is new in Vaughan is the actuality and sensuous quality which pulls our feelings closer to his.

The structure of these 'paragraph poems' is of experience, meditation and prayer. The last quarter of this poem is a prayer for the spiritual consolation the poet's religion can provide:

> And now the spirit, not the dust
>   Must be thy brother.
> Yet I have one *Pearle* by whose light
>   All things I see,

> And in the heart of Earth, and night
>> Find Heaven, and thee.

Language can hardly get simpler or more mysterious. Blake, not Wordsworth, is the Romantic whose impact is similar. As with Blake, the mystery derives from the vagueness or ambiguity of images as in a dream. The pearl may be the spirit of his brother, or his wife, or his faith, or the Bible.

The contrast with Herbert is striking. In the earlier poet's great religious poems such as 'Mortification', the standpoint is the pulpit, the purpose is doctrinal and the hero is 'man':

> Man, ere he is aware,
>> Hath put together a solemnitie,
>>> And drest his herse, while he has breath
>>>> As yet to spare:
>>> Yet Lord, instruct us so to die,
>>> That all these dyings may be life in death.

In this poem, when the reader is moved by an image close to his life, like baby-clothes or bed or music, or dressing a hearse; or challenged into involvement by some surprising feat of concision like moving 'within the circle of his breath' or 'put together a solemnitie', he is being shown a commonplace of medieval church doctrine in a new way, not the private ejaculations of a desolate soul. Twenty years changed everything utterly. The Royalist poet in exile is driven towards new poetic qualities: a different kind of actuality and an urgently sensuous account of his personal experience. His imagery reflects not only his reading but also the glistening hill country of the Silures and of his childhood, into which he had retreated:

> Stars are of mighty use: The night
>> Is dark and long;
> The Rode foul, and where one goes right
>> Six may go wrong.

> One twinkling ray
> Shot oe'r some cloud
> May clear much way
> And gain a croud.

When Vaughan's countryside is compared with the gardens and meadows of Marvell's pastorals, one quickly feels the difference between the sheltered unreal world of classical idyll and the fresh hills and fields, the dew, the dark, the sheep and the flowers in Vaughan's Wales.

The unwillingness to acknowledge and value the originality of Vaughan may stem from the difficulty in categorising him. Like Purcell, he is both the last voice of a dying culture and the first of a new one.

Vaughan *is* a metaphysical. His 'Ring' is of pure and endless light, but it is also the bridegroom's present for his bride. Themes are abstract, and controlled by traditional structures of meditation, argument and prayer. The pervading theme is the progress of the soul. Poems present little scenes and often there is a development of attitude in the course of the scene. Vaughan's first lines often have the arresting impact of Donne's, although more subdued.

'Subdued' is the key. The world of Court and Church has been destroyed and Vaughan is a refugee. His world is remote and private: his experience of grief is real. Images are rooted both in the Authorised Bible and in Welsh scenery. His music is quiet. More than in any other seventeenth-century poet, one feels that it is the product and the account of actual experience.

AFTERTHOUGHTS

1

Do you agree that 'Donne is always a more exciting poet than Vaughan' (page 70)?

2

Do you agree that it can be 'insensitive' to 'judge one metaphysical poet against another' (page 73)?

3

Do you agree with Cairns's distinction between the *description* and the *expression* of emotion (page 74)?

4

To what extent do you agree that the word 'subdued' (page 77) is 'the key' to Vaughan?

Pat Pinsent

Pat Pinsent is Principal Lecturer in English at the Roehampton Institute.

ESSAY

Form and meaning in Donne and Herbert

The relationship between the way in which something is said and the meaning it is conveying is one which has varied in different periods of literature. For the sixteenth- or seventeenth-century writer, this kind of relationship is particularly close, so that how a poem is written is usually organically linked to what the poet is communicating. This idea may be reflected in many different ways; the writer of an epic, like Milton in *Paradise Lost*, feels the need to use dignified language and a suitable form, such as blank verse. A quite different choice is that of the shape of a cross for a poem on Christ's crucifixion by the obscure seventeenth-century writer, Nathaniel Richards.

The writers included in Helen Gardner's anthology *The Metaphysical Poets* often reveal a detached concern about the appropriateness of the form they choose. As Gardner writes in her Introduction:

> The metaphysical poets favoured either very simple verse forms, octosyllabic couplets or quatrains, or else stanzas created for the particular poem, in which length of line and rhyme scheme artfully enforced the sense.

> (p. 19)

I do not propose to give much attention here to the 'very simple verse forms', which are more characteristic of the work of some of the other poets than they are of either Donne or Herbert. Many of Donne's poems, such as the early Elegies and Satyres, and the Holy Sonnets of his *Songs and Sonets* on which much of his fame rests provide ample evidence to support the second part of the above quotation, as does nearly all of Herbert's work. Yet even within the work of two writers who both showed an outstanding degree of boldness in choice of form, there are significant differences in approach which enable the reader, almost before even reading a poem, to decide whether it is by Donne or by Herbert.

A glance at any selection of the poems of these writers immediately conveys the impression of Donne's text often being more packed on to the page than Herbert's. This is partly because Donne makes more use of the regular longer line, the iambic pentameter, than Herbert does, but it is also true in poems where he invents his own stanza form, as in most of his *Songs and Sonets*. The impression is often given that the speaker or persona of the poem (who should not necessarily be identified with Donne himself) is involved in a dramatic dialogue with his mistress, where she is given the opportunity to answer back, though her replies are inaudible to us. It was an age when the drama was generally written in the ten-syllable iambic line, which provided the norm from which variations in line length and metrical stress would depart. It is perhaps hardly surprising therefore that Donne, a great frequenter of the theatre in his youth, should tend to start from a longish line unit.

If we look briefly at one or two poems, we can see how the interaction of line length and rhyme pattern in reinforcing meaning works. In 'The Flea' we have a stanza of alternating eight- and ten-syllable lines, with an additional final ten-syllable. The rhyme pattern is as simple as possible: *aabbccddd* — four sets of successive rhymes (which cannot be described as couplets because of the unequal line length) and a final additional rhyming line. The result of this very conclusive end to the stanzas is to set them apart from each other in a way similar to the acts of a play; between the first and the second, the imagined addressee, the woman who is resisting his amorous pleas, threatens to kill the flea, and between the second and the third she actually kills it.

Another very well known poem, 'The Sunne Rising', provides more variation between long and short lines but still reveals a preponderance of ten-syllabled lines; in terms of syllables the pattern is: 8, 4, 10, 10, 8, 8, 10, 10, 10, 10, with a rhyme pattern *abbacdcdee*. This time the ostensible addressee is the sun, though the implied audience is the woman who is thus valued above the riches of the world, as well as the intended audience of readers, who may feel that they, like the sun, are intruding on a couple in bed. Nevertheless, the poet, by the actual writing of the poem, has invited them to the scene. The reason for the invitation is partly to share the delight of the speaker in his mistress's beauty, but also, I suspect, to admire the cleverness of the logic. The effect of the longer lines and the couplet at the end of each stanza is again to mark the divisions in a logical argument very closely related to the evocation of setting. With Donne, drama and logic are frequently very closely linked. The effect of the verse form here could be claimed to be that we are drawn in gently by the shorter lines at the beginning, we reach a partial completion of thought by the longer pair which follow; there is then a transition in the shorter lines in the middle of the stanza, followed by the full working out of the logic in the culmination in the four longer lines, concluding in the couplet. The separate blocks of this argument are at the same time united by the similar form of the stanzas and divided by the emphatic endings of each verse.

Not all of Donne's poems are so clearly divided up into this kind of long, individually tailored stanza. Occasionally, unlike Herbert, he makes use of the quatrain, and when he does, notably in 'The Extasie' and 'A Valediction: forbidding mourning', he seems more prone to create a continuous structure with strong links of meaning between one verse and another. In the latter poem, we have a good deal of use of cohesive ties. The first two verses are linked by the 'As' of the simile and the 'So' which shows its application, and later in the poem we have many other conjunctions which tie the argument together: 'But' (verse 3, l.3), 'But' (verse 5, l.1), 'therefore' (verse 6, l.1), 'If' (verse 7, l.1), 'And though' (verse 8, l.1), and 'Such' (verse 9, l.1). I would suggest that this kind of cohesive argument would be virtually impossible in the much more separated format of the stanzas of the poems previously discussed.

My contention therefore is that the kind of stanza which

Donne creates, in these and many other poems, is organically linked to the movement of the action between the persona and the implied other participant(s). The choice of line length and rhyme pattern appears to be part of this overall concept, subsumed to the main idea of the poem.

When we turn to the poetry of Herbert, we are immediately struck by the more open appearance of many pages. While some of Herbert's poems do use a longer line, notably his relatively few sonnets, there is a more abundant use of very short lines. The variety of form in Herbert's major work, *The Temple*, is immense, and seldom if ever is the same pattern used twice. Clearly some of this must represent (whatever devout rationalisation the poet made to himself!) sheer delight in technical virtuosity, but I doubt if the choice of form is ever entirely accidental.

In some well-known cases, of course, it is relatively easy to see Herbert's intention. 'Easter-wings' is an example of a poem deliberately written in a shape, like (and much better than) the one by Richards mentioned earlier. Where the lesser writer seems to have done little more than ask his printer to chop the lines into shape, Herbert deliberately makes use of the idea of wings throughout his poem. The universal loss of the Fall (verse 1) and the personal decline (verse 2) are mirrored by the lessening lines; the shortest lines are: 'Most poore' and 'Most thinne', and as the poet images rising and flight the lines grow likewise. It is a measure of Herbert's achievement that what could have been little more than arithmetic has been transformed into a powerful poem.

Another famous illustration of Herbert's technique is 'Deniall', where he images the disorder in the breast (verse 1) with a lack of final rhyme and a discordance of metre throughout the first five stanzas, only resolving the situation in stanza six. Here, with a reinforcement of the image of music (previously invoked with the negative images 'untun'd, unstrung' (verse 5)) and with a change to regular metre, he arrives at the rhyme our ears have been anticipating from the beginning:

> They and my minde may chime,
> And mend my ryme.

Several other poems would repay closer attention than it is

possible to give them here. The irregularity of 'The Collar', for example, with the first four lines having ten, four, eight and ten syllables and no discernible overall pattern of either line length or rhyme throughout, mirrors the apparent rebellion which is brought to order in the alternate rhyming of the last four lines by the one word *'Child'* and the simple acknowledgement *'My Lord'*.

The alternate longer and shorter lines in 'Love' are particularly appropriate to the interchange between speakers within the dialogue mode, reinforced by the *ababcc* rhyme pattern of the three verses. There is no sense of separation between the stanzas; in fact the argument continues with the last line of each verse being answered by the first line of the next — a continuation which is made easier by the inconclusive short lines which end the first two verses. The poet does however achieve a final effect even with the short line at the end of stanza three because a simple statement replaces the questions of the other stanzas, and provides a cessation to the restless movement of the poem in 'So I did sit and eat'.

In 'Aaron', the words ending the lines are the same within each verse: 'head', 'breast', 'dead', 'rest', 'drest', five times, while the content of the verses changes totally. This images the way the human is transformed in Christ and reinforces the meaning emphatically. Many more instances of Herbert uniting meaning and form could be given, both from poems in Gardner's anthology and from those in the complete work (notably 'The Church Floor', 'Church Monuments', 'The Altar', 'Paradise', 'Sinnes Round').

The impression derived from a study of these poems is that as well as producing more variety than Donne, Herbert generates the sense of what could be described as a 'sacred game'. He seems to be choosing an incident from his spiritual autobiography, an experience of prayer, the realisation of the gulf between his own unworthiness and the immense goodness of God, and trying to think of a form he has not previously used which would be the best kind of picture frame to put it into. There is a drama, but because the other actor in it is always the same, God, not the different mistresses hypothesised by Donne, it is as if all the poems are part of the same drama, not a series of individual playlets like Donne's poems. The poet, bearing in mind the command to become as a little child and always very conscious of God's parenthood (as is evident in 'The Collar'), seems to be playing before God in his invention of these new forms.

Even the way the two poets use the sonnet differs. Donne consistently chooses a Petrarchan form of the octet (*abbaabba*) and although there are some variations in the sestet, there is always a final couplet, which seems essential to convey the force of his argument. Any variations he uses have already been authenticated by their use by Sidney in his sequence *Astrophel and Stella* (first published 1591). Herbert, on the other hand, eschews any existing form but seems to play with the sonnet (which in any case is a word game in itself). In 'Redemption' and 'Prayer', he starts as if he were going to use the Shakespearean form (*ababcdcd*) but then changes to something more like the Petrarchan in the sestet (*effegg*). Various tentative explanations could be put forward for this. I would ignore the possibility that he couldn't meet the more stringent rhyme requirements of the Petrarchan mode! Rather, I would suggest that he is deliberately removing the possibility of partial closure that the couplets within the octet of this form provide, while seeking closure, by contrast, within the sestet before the end as well as within the final couplet. By this change, he is employing the movement of the Shakespearean form within the first eight lines, but uniting with it the transition between the octet and the sestet, characteristic of the Petrarchan, so that a development in the argument is reflected by the form. It is, however, perhaps worthy of remark that Herbert's sonnet form does not appear to have caught on widely even among poets most influenced by him.

I propose to finish by looking more closely at a single poem by each of these poets, in the attempt to show how their strengths are revealed in their manipulation of the form, and to examine the kinds of differences between them which I have suggested. Donne's 'A Valediction: of Weeping' and Herbert's 'The Pulley' are both fairly short (27 and 20 lines, with three nine-line stanzas and four five-line ones respectively). Donne's poem has line lengths of 4, 10, 10, 10, 4, 4, 10, 10, 14 syllables, with a rhyme pattern *abbaccddd*. Herbert's stanzas have 6, 10, 10, 10, 6 syllables, and a rhyme pattern of *ababa*. Here already, before we look at the meaning, we can see how the surface differences between the two writers are revealed. While Donne does make use here of several very short lines, his stanzas end in alexandrines, which provide a very adequate barrier between the three separate parts into which his argument, again set into a dramatic situation, is divided. Herbert's stanzas, ending in a short line, tend to make the argument cohesive, and the poet uses link words, similar to those Donne employs in 'A Valediction: forbidding mourning' which were discussed earlier. The second, third and fourth stanzas start with 'So', 'For' and 'Yet', which cohere with the initial 'When' to provide a single development of thought.

It could be argued that 'A Valediction: of Weeping' is one of the nearest poems that Donne ever produced to the tradition of writing in a shape. The first four lines could resemble the tear gathering in the eye, the two short ones its fall, and the last three its dispersal on the surface where it arrives. I have no means of knowing whether this was what Donne intended but there is no doubt of the visual nature of the images: the tear becomes a coin, a nothing, a globe, a destructive flood, an example to the sea...The imagined presence of his mistress is important, for she is presumably continuing weeping, as well as sighing in the last verse, and thus giving material for the ingenuity of the persona to work on. Thus, rather like 'The Flea', the poem depends on action by the silent but present addressee. This gives some of the emotional force to what could have become a mere exercise in wit.

Instead of having God as addressee, as in most of his poems, in 'The Pulley' Herbert provides an anecdote, a mini-creation-myth accounting for the restlessness of humankind, with God as speaker and no action intervening between stanzas to interrupt the account. As in 'Love', the problem Herbert is faced with is that of providing closure within a pattern where the short line at the end of each stanza has been a means of leading the argument on. How do we know we've arrived? A good deal is achieved by the use of sounds; for most of the poem these are far from smooth, with a particularly frequent use of 'r' towards the end, contrasted however with a build-up of emphasis on the 's' sound. Partly, however, Herbert achieves the rest we require by the title of the poem, never explicitly mentioned within the text. We are to imagine the movement with all these other goods pulling down on one side and thus forcing the other side up, presumably with increasing speed, until at the end the human is tossed to God. There's nowhere else to go, so the poem has to end!

In both poems there is a fairly subtle relationship between the rhyme, the line length, and the meaning. In Donne's poem, the initial flow of the tears is suggested after the first short line by the three longer lines which follow. The roundness of the tear and its readiness to fall seem to me to be suggested by the very short rhyming lines, while the three longer lines all rhyming imply a sense of finality with nothing further that is positive coming out of the situation. In the second and the third stanzas, Donne seems to create the effect of setting an image up for the reader's consideration ('a round ball', a 'Moone') before developing the idea more fully in the longer lines succeeding it. In each case the shorter rhymed lines mark a transition in thought, while near the end, the rhyme 'winde'/'finde', using what would at that date have been consistently a long 'i', gives an almost onomatopoeic quality when it is echoed in the prevalence of 'i's again in the last three lines. The other repeated sound near the end is 'th', not only in the threefold rhyme but also in 'thou', 'anothers' and 'others', again reinforcing the emotive effect of the final word, 'death'. The absurd hyperbole of the final stanza, seeing tears and sighs as a threat to life, is made acceptable by the way the poet has imperceptibly guided our reactions by technical devices like rhyme.

'The Pulley' also, as might be expected, makes good use of technique. The symmetrical form of the stanzas, with first and fifth lines of equal length surrounding the others, and a rhyme scheme which emphasises this, is appropriate for a symmetrical device such as a pulley where the force on one side is (ideally) the image of that on the other. In the first verse, the poet contrasts a sense of largesse in the riches with the smallness of humanity in the final short line, 'Contract into a span'. In the second stanza we have again the contrast between the abundance that has flowed from God and the single gift remaining, which is pinpointed by the shorter line. A similar pattern informs the remaining stanzas, extra force always being given to the meaning of the last line. The nature of the rhymes adds to the effect, for in stanzas two and three, there is a contrast between the monosyllabic rhymes in the first, third and fifth lines and the two-syllabled 'pleasure'/'treasure', 'creature'/ 'Nature' in the lines with which they alternate. This seems to me to maintain the awareness of the conflict between stability and motion, continued also in the contrast between the rhyming three-syllabled words 'restlesnesse' and 'wearinesse' and the other three monosyllabic rhymes in the final verse: 'rest' (the key word of the poem), 'least' (pronounced with a short vowel) and 'breast', the home of humanity in God.

It could be argued that the rhyme and patterning in 'The Pulley' is less 'playful' than in some of the other Herbert poems which I have discussed. The sense of the poet as childlike, at play before God, is not, however, lost, for he knows that we realise that the little story he tells is not literally true and that he has not heard God saying these words. The 'sacred game' continues.

These two very different poems, like the other Donne and Herbert poems which have been considered more briefly, do indeed show the writers utilising all the resources of rhyme and line length at their disposal to reinforce their meanings. They show us how, in the hands of great poets, technique, which can seem contrived and laboured in the hands of lesser writers, can blend in with meaning to form an organic whole, of which the effect often seems so natural that the reader finds it difficult to imagine the possibility that is could have been otherwise than it is.

AFTERTHOUGHTS

1

Why is blank verse regarded as 'a suitable form' for an epic poem?

2

What relationship does Pinsent suggest between the dramatic content of Donne's poetry and its form (pages 80–82)?

3

Is it helpful to think of *The Temple* as a 'sacred game' (page 83)?

4

How important is it for a poem to sound 'natural' (page 87)?

Michael Gearin-Tosh

Michael Gearin-Tosh is Fellow and Tutor in English Literature at St Catherine's College, Oxford. He is also Associate Director of the Oxford School of Drama.

ESSAY

Marvell and Horace: 'An Horatian Ode'

There has been a debate for at least fifty years about 'An Horatian Ode'. The issue, put very simply, is who Marvell supports. Is he for Cromwell, the revolutionary hero, who 'cast the Kingdoms old/ Into another mould' (ll.35–36)? Or is Marvell's heart with Charles I, the anointed king who, at his execution, 'nothing common did or mean/ Upon that memorable Scene' (ll.57–58)? Powerful arguments are made on either side. Yet there are further questions which can be asked. Is Marvell for both? Is he for neither? Is the poem less about the historical protagonists than about the values implied by Marvell's meditative detachments? A clue is given by the title.

It was not common to call a poem 'An Horatian Ode'. Neither Donne nor Ben Jonson, the fathers of seventeenth-century verse, did so. But educated men and women at the time read Horace. They would recall, as Marvell recalls, his famous ode on the victory of Augustus over Cleopatra (the victory which Shakespeare dramatises in *Antony and Cleopatra*). Here is a translation made some thirty years after Marvell's poem by Thomas Creech (1659–1700):

> Now, now, 'tis time to dance and play,
> And drink, and frolick all the Day;

'Tis time, my Friends, to banish Care;
    And costly Feasts
With thankful Hearts prepare   5
In hallow'd Shrines, and make the Gods your Guests.

'Twas Treason once to sport a Flask,
And Sin to pierce the noble Cask,
Whilst nought but boading Fears were seen
        For Ills to come;   10
    When *Egypt's* haughty Queen
With wither'd Eunuchs threaten'd mighty *Rome*:

A Woman vain, whose Hopes could rise
To such impossibilities!
A Woman drunk with sweet success;   15
        Whom smiling Fate
    Had brought to dare no less
Than *Cesar*'s Fortune, and the *Roman* State.

But soon her Pride to Fears retir'd,
When all her Ships were sunk or fir'd;   20
And real Dread possess'd her Mind,
        When *Cesar*'s Oars
    Did press so close behind,
And bore his Navy to the frighted Shores,

(As Hawks pursue the trembling Doves,   25
Thro' open Fields or shady Groves;
Or as swift Huntsmen chace the Deer
        Thro' *Thracian* Plains,
    That fly as wing'd with fear)
To bring the fatal Monster into Chains.   30

But She design'd a nobler Fate,
And falling would appear as great
As when She singly fill'd the Throne;
        No Fears betray'd,
    Nor fled to Coasts unknown   35
To live secure, or meanly beg for Aid.

Her falling Throne with smiling look
She boldly saw; she dar'd provoke
Fierce Serpents rough with poys'nous trains,

To dart their Tongue,   40
And fill her dying Veins;
Grown furious now on Death resolv'd so long:

The stout *Liburnian* Ships, the Fame
And lasting glory of her Shame,
She envy'd; she, a Soul too proud,   45
Too haughty to be seen
Amongst the private Crowd,
And grace a Triumph less than *Egypt*'s Queen.

Both Horace and Marvell open their poems with statements about the present, calling attention to the present moment more than once. Afterwards both poets discuss 'impossibilities' (Creech, 1.14). Cleopatra dared 'Cesar's Fortune, and the Roman State'. Similarly, Cromwell sought and gained the head of Charles I, interestingly called 'Caesar's head' (1.23); and he overthrew the English state, its monarchy and constitution, when he ruined 'the great Work of Time' (1.34). Cromwell succeeded and Cleopatra did not, so that later in Marvell's poem, the echoes are of Caesar and not of the Queen. Cromwell is a hawk pursuing its prey in lines 91–96. And he is a hunter who, like Caesar, chases deer in lines 105–112.

These allusions mean that, for seventeenth-century readers, Horace's poem was part of the experience of reading 'An Horatian Ode' and we should ask what this involved.

Horace was so magnanimous a writer that, as a great classical scholar has written, 'at the end of a poem written to celebrate Cleopatra's defeat, her greatness dominates over everything else' (Eduard Fraenkel, *Horace*, 1957, reprinted 1980, p. 160). Horace was a Roman and he believed that Caesar's triumph averted a disaster. His description of Cleopatra in verse five is damning: *fatale monstrum*, Creech's 'fatal Monster' (1.30), refers to 'something outside the norm of nature, something at which we look with wonder and often with horror' (Fraenkel, p. 160). There is horror, for example, in the grotesqueness of a tyranny which is run through 'wither'd Eunuchs' (1.12): the original Latin is even more gruesome. Yet, as the poem continues, horror is replaced by wonder — and noble wonder — at Cleopatra's resilience. The monster becomes a woman in as few words, a vulnerable lady reduced either to fugitive and primitive exile or to humiliation if she is to live. She chooses suicide and with fierce magnificence, almost greed. Horace's ode begins with a dance and ends, unexpectedly, with an element of tragic joy.

What of Marvell? Horace celebrates Rome's victory over a great threat. Marvell's full title is 'An *Horatian* Ode upon *Cromwel's* Return from *Ireland*'. The rebellion of the Irish in 1641 was a catalyst for the tensions which exploded in the English Civil War of 1642–45. Now, in 1651, Cromwell has at last defeated the rebels. But there is little sense of rejoicing in 'An Horatian Ode'. Horace's ode starts with a thrusting, excited rhythm, the beat of joyful dance — more evident in the original Latin than in Creech. In sharp contrast, Marvell starts with an elegy for the forsaken muses, their groves and the young man's abandoned books.

There is also a change in the figure who dominates the poem. At first Cromwell is, like Cleopatra, a prodigy outside nature. He is a gigantic bolt of lightning which destroys 'palaces and temples' and can even blast through laurel which was reputed to ward off lightning (ll.21–24). He is a 'climacteric' (l.104), a massive turning point in the history of nations. Marvell also describes his personal qualities. Cromwell has shown 'industrious Valour' (l.33), courage (ll.45–46), astuteness (ll.47–52) and constitutional propriety (ll.81–96). These are scarcely characteristics which lead to tragedy, but they are the qualities of panegyric. And panegyric has its own type of joy. If 'An Horatian Ode' modulated to that, there would be an equivalent of the warmth of Horace's ending.

We have a yardstick in this regard since Marvell did write a panegyric on Cromwell five years after 'An Horatian Ode'. Cromwell's personal qualities are again set against his political role, but both are significantly changed:

> For neither didst thou from the first apply
> Thy sober spirit unto things too high,
> But in thine own fields exercised'st long,
> An healthful mind within a body strong;
> Till at the seventh time thou in the skies,
> As a small cloud, like a man's hand, didst rise;
> Then did thick mists and winds the air deform,
> And down at last thou poured'st the fertile storm,

Which to the thirsty land did plenty bring,
But, though forewarned, o'ertook and wet the King.

('The First Anniversary', ll.229–238)

The Civil War is a storm in both poems but the stupendous lightning of 'An Horatian Ode' has become 'fertile' rain to a 'thirsty land'. There is a strong biblical allusion to the rain of 1 Kings 18, whereas the universe of 'An Horatian Ode' seems to be resolutely pagan if not godless, dominated by Fate, the gloomy, impersonal power which overrules all in Virgil. In 'The First Anniversary' Cromwell's personal qualities are his 'sober spirit' and the exercise of 'an healthful mind'. 'Healthful' has connotations of moral and spiritual welfare, that growth of temperance and loving charity which comes only from inner exercise. It is far from Cromwell's manipulative temperament in 'An Horatian Ode':

And *Hampton* shows what part
He had of wiser Art,
Where, twining subtile fears with hope...

(ll.47–49)

'The First Anniversary' may be too idyllic a picture of heroism, at least in this section, but it throws into relief the *realpolitik* of 'An Horatian Ode'.

A crucial factor in the interpretation of a poem is its shape, and the shape of 'An Horatian Ode' has been neglected by critics. The poem begins and ends with scenes, the first an intimate vignette, the second a majestic tableau. The imaginative pressure of the work invites us to compare them with each other. Both scenes focus on a single person. In both, advice is offered. Both contain shade, the youth's 'shadows', Cromwell's 'shady night'. And both contain a reference to the arts. The first scene includes the muses and books, and is dismissed with a contrast between them and 'the inglorious Arts of Peace' (l.10). The final scene ends with the aphorism which concludes the poem, an aphorism which was traditional even in its wording:

The same *Arts* that did *gain*
A *Pow'r* must it *maintain*.

(ll.119–120)

It is the difference between the scenes which is arresting. Although both concentrate on a single person, the youth is solitary but Cromwell is isolated. The youth chooses to be alone for the solitude of artistic creation. His 'shadows' are the trees and groves among which poetry was held to flourish in the classical world. He is somewhat like the thinker in Marvell's poem 'The Garden':

> Annihilating all that's made
> To a green Thought in a green Shade.
>
> (ll.47–48)

But Cromwell is alone because people are hiding. The Scots are visually annihilating themselves in the 'tufted brake', hoping their plaids will conceal them. Cromwell's isolation is paradoxical in that he is at the head of an army. Where is the companionship of his fellow-soldiers? They are described as 'hounds', mere implements of war. The man who 'Did thorough his own Side/ His fiery way divide' (ll.15–16), seems to be paying the price in not having friends or colleagues.

The final lines of the poem contain a reference to Homer which is recognised by scholars but scarcely interpreted:

> And for the last effect
> Still keep thy Sword erect:
> Besides the force it has to fright
> The Spirits of the shady Night . . .
>
> (ll.116–119)

In Book XI of *The Odyssey*, Odysseus makes blood sacrifices in order to summon the dead. As ghosts flock round, he draws his sword to keep them away until Teiresias, the great prophet, comes to reveal the future. The difference between Homer and Marvell is one of motivation. Both Odysseus and Cromwell draw their swords in order to frighten the spirits. But Odysseus keeps the spirits back to prevent them drinking the blood so that enough will be left to give Teiresias the strength to speak to him. Cromwell frightens them as an end in itself. For Odysseus:

> . . . the communication
> Of the dead is tongued with fire beyond the language of the
> living.
>
> (T S Eliot, 'Little Gidding', ll.50–51)

His aim is communication, Cromwell's aim is intimidation. Nor has Cromwell summoned these spirits of the dead: they haunt him, like the ghosts of those unjustly killed who haunt Richard III and Macbeth in Shakespeare.

This exclusion of communication is perhaps the most interesting link between the vignette which opens the poem and its concluding tableau. For the youth is also portrayed with spirits. They are none less than the muses, who, like his art, his poetry and his books are concerned to communicate. But all are dismissed in line 10 as part of the 'inglorious Arts of Peace' through the pressure of Cromwell's ambition. This anticipates the relationship of the final tableau to the opening scene. The tableau is destroying the vignette, at least driving it into obscurity and irrelevance: the 'forward' youth will 'now' make no mark in the world by poetry. The age which valued art is over.

Do we prefer the new age with its world of lightning, nets, bleeding heads, hawks, dogs, and the dominating symbol of an erect sword? Cromwell's greatness is purchased at a price. Marvell's tone is not partisan. That is alien to the Horatian manner. 'Much to the Man is due' wrote Marvell, and the poem declares much. The reader can turn it into a panegyric of Cromwell if he insists. But the wording of Marvell's phrase suggests that certain things are not due to Cromwell. The poem also indicates those. In addition, the allusion to Horace's ode makes for wary and alert reading. Horace begins with a domestic scene and ends, like Marvell, with a hero. But there the resemblance ends. Cleopatra draws us to her in human admiration and sympathy: Cromwell makes us withdraw, even hide, from a fearsome, military dominance. Horace starts with rare wine being brought out for a celebration, Marvell starts with things being put away. A bleaker age has come. And it is likely to continue.

At the end of his discussion of Horace's ode, Fraenkel observed:

> The magnanimity with which the defeated queen is extolled should not be taken as an isolated phenomenon. It springs from that deep respect for dignity in man's behaviour which the Greeks, though they did not, of course, always practise it, at any rate held up to themselves as an ideal. And as an ideal it took root in the Roman mind, whose hardy, if somewhat dry, nature

proved fertile for the growth of some of the finest plants from the garden of Greek ethics. The rulers of the world came to recognize that you ought not to humiliate your defeated enemy, and that by trying to degrade him you will in fact degrade yourself.

... it is a fact, and a very important fact indeed, that the poets, voicing what was in the minds of the best men, could, without fear of disapproval, treat the defeated enemy in such a manner at the moment when a life-and-death struggle had been decided. In the later history of mankind it may not often have happened that a victory of similar magnitude was glorified in a poem so jubilant and at the same time so profoundly humane as the ode *Nunc est bibendum.*

In 'An Horatian Ode' Marvell focuses upon this decline in humanity as 'arts' of cunning and violence, sinister parodies, squeeze out the arts which celebrate and help to guarantee the true dignity of a society.

AFTERTHOUGHTS

1

Explain the importance to Gearin-Tosh's argument of the translation which opens this essay (pages 89–91).

2

What do you understand by *realpolitik* (page 93)?

3

Do you agree with Gearin-Tosh's interpretation of the role of the 'solitary' youth (page 94)? How else might this figure be interpreted?

4

'Marvell's tone is not partisan' (page 95): Compare Gearin-Tosh's arguments in this essay with Holderness's view (pages 20–31).

D

David Lewis

*David Lewis is Director of English
Studies at Barton Peveril College,
Hampshire. He is a Chief Examiner for
AS-level English.*

ESSAY

Drama in Donne and Herbert

John Donne (1572–1631) was almost an exact contemporary of
Shakespeare (1564–1616). Their literary careers both began in
the 1590s, a decade which saw a great and exciting flowering of
the drama in London — drama written mostly in poetry and
often of great wit. Donne was a student of the Inns of Court, and
Shakespeare was much admired (particularly for *Love's Labour's
Lost*) by the 'termers', as the law students were known. Moreover, Donne, as a young man, was described as a 'visitor of
ladies, *frequenter of plays*, and writer of conceited verses'. It
would surely be more surprising if we did *not* find dramatic
qualities in Donne's poetry than if we did. It is interesting to
note that some of his early poems were much admired by the
dramatist Ben Jonson, who was born in the same year as Donne.

The audience that Donne wrote for at the beginning of his
career was not the general public, but young men of his own age
and education — a group that formed a small but significant
section of the contemporary theatre audience. The strong element
of exhibitionism, of shock and surprise at all costs, of great
extravagance, can clearly be seen in the drama of the period. For
Donne actually to write for the stage — for players — would
have been rather beneath his dignity, but his poetry certainly
contains striking dramatic qualities, and he was able to syn-
thesise the essence of drama into his work.

The term 'drama' is notoriously difficult to define, but I shall use it in two major senses in this essay: first, to include aspects of plays written for the stage, with situations or settings in which persons speak in character, usually with some development of the situation; and secondly to cover the use of language that has a particularly striking impact, vividness or force, and frequently exaggeration.

One of the most noticeable features of Donne's poetry is that almost every word of it is 'spoken' in the first person, mostly by a male voice, and mostly as monologue. ('Breake of Day' and 'Confined Love' are both spoken by a woman, Elegie XI has two interruptions by the mistress, and some of the Satyres have good dialogue — especially I and IV — but these are exceptions.) It is important to realise that this use of the spoken voice is a dramatic treatment, not to be confused with Donne's own voice, any more than Othello or Hamlet should be regarded as the voice of Shakespeare himself (though some critics have in the past come close to doing that). Just as a dramatist creates characters by drawing on a mixture of imagination and of personal experience, so does Donne, and once we accept that in his poems characters are speaking 'in role', then some apparent problems disappear, particularly the question of sincerity, which becomes irrelevant. A difficulty is that most of us are still imbued with a 'Romantic' view of poetry, and expect it to reflect the genuine ideas or feelings of the writer. Because of this, many students find it hard to come to terms with Donne, who appears to be a misogynistic chauvinist one moment and a tender lover the next. However, there is still a complication, even if we see the poetry as drama, for some of the poems of mutual love seem so compelling that I find it difficult not to see them as representing Donne's genuine feelings towards his wife (and therefore written after the marriage in 1601). But since we do not know for certain the occasion or date of any of the *Songs and Sonets*, we should always be on our guard, and not see the speaker's voice as identical with Donne's own.

A very striking role is that of the cynic. 'The Indifferent' sees truth as a vice — 'I can love any, so she be not true'. 'Woman's Constancy' portrays an extremely cynical male character (though denying virtue equally to man and woman): 'Now thou hast lov'd me one whole day', as if this is remarkable in itself, 'To morrow *when* thou leav'st, what wilt thou say?', the assumption being that no two people could possibly endure more than twenty-four hours together. In the Song 'Goe, and catche a falling starre' the male chauvinist assumes there is no constantly faithful woman in the world, but the gaiety of the ending with its tripping metre suggests the insouciance of this view. The last two lines of 'Communitie':

> And when hee hath the kernell eate,
> Who doth not fling away the shell?

are insulting with their conviction that no woman is worthy of a man's fidelity. In 'Confined Love', on the other hand, we are presented with a similar view from the opposite sex. Here the woman complains against the injustice of 'man's' law that women should be confined to a single man. It is natural to desire novelty and change, in which lie the only true freedom:

> Good is not good, unlesse
> A thousand it possesse

The enjoyment of such poems lies in their sheer outrageousness, in the entertaining way in which they present an untenable position with such conviction. They are, in a sense, dramatic exercises.

Another role that we observe in a number of poems is that of the constant male lover who rebukes the woman for her lack of truth. Sometimes this voice is sad, as in 'The Legacie', and sometimes powerfully vindictive and seeking revenge, as in 'The Apparition', where the man wants to make the woman who has slighted him — the 'murdresse' — suffer after his death. He gloats over the prospect of haunting her and of seeing her desiring more than being desired, with her lover shrinking from her in a 'false sleepe'. In 'Twicknam Garden' the voice is one of misery. The suffering lover implores:

> Make me a mandrake, so I may grow here,
> Or a stone fountaine weeping out my yeare.

The view of the woman is again insulting, for she is true only to be cruel and bring about his death.

Very different from the role of the unrequited lover is that of the lover whose love is reciprocated. Poems of mutual love are extremely rare in poetry but Donne wrote several of them. Even within this narrow band, however, there are constant changes of mood and attitude, often within a single poem. In 'The Sunne Rising', for example, the speaker is at first angry to be woken, then rather contemptuous as he pities the sun for being less powerful than himself, and finally concerned to ease the burden of the sun in its old age. The expression of love in these poems is often ostentatiously effusive:

> Only our love hath no decay
>
> > ('The Anniversarie')

> And wee were mutuall Elements to us,
> > And made of one another
> > > ('The Dissolution')

and sometimes very moving, as in the valedictory poems, particularly in 'A Valediction: of Weeping', with the tenderness of the man pouring forth his tears before the woman, and her responding likewise. The role in 'Farewell to Love', however, is totally different again, being that of an embittered older man rejecting love and sex as hollow fleeting pleasures.

Apart from 'A Nocturnall upon S. Lucies day', which was possibly written for Lucy, Countess of Bedford, none of the *Songs and Sonets*, unlike the Verse Letters, is clearly addressed to an actual person (though some of the poems of mutual love were almost certainly influenced by his wife, if not written to her). By adopting the dramatic device of characters speaking in role, Donne has given himself great artistic freedom and has achieved a surprising range and variety of approach.

Not every poem is addressed to a woman. 'The Blossome', for example, is addressed first to a flower, then to the man's heart, which is allowed to reply. 'The Sunne Rising' is addressed to the sun, 'A Jet Ring sent' to the ring, and 'The Will', 'Love's Exchange' and 'Love's Usury' are all addressed to the God of Love. The last of these, like 'The Indifferent', is a boastful monologue proclaiming a cheekily cynical attitude to the world in general — he will even love a constant woman later if given a free youth now. The voice of Venus is heard in the third stanza of 'The Indifferent' and in 'The Flea' Donne uses reported speech for the woman's reply. The religious poems, of course, differ from the secular poems in that Donne's own voice is speaking in them, but even in these he achieves dramatic effects of dialogue. 'Good Friday, 1613. Riding Westward', for example, begins philosophically, but becomes dramatic as Donne addresses Christ, turning his back in the action of the poem to receive corrections. The ending has a powerful dramatic effect:

> Restore thine Image, so much, by thy grace,
> That thou may'st know mee, and I'll turne my face.

In a play of course we expect the characters to exist in a context, usually an actual setting, although many of Shakespeare's scenes have very vague locations. In some of Donne's poems there is no clear setting in physical terms, but rather a situation in dramatic terms — of 'man addressing woman'. In many, however, the characters are placed in an explicit setting which greatly enhances the dramatic effect. Donne is fond, for example, of scenes in or around a bed, and typically these display a great variety of approaches. The bed can be the setting, not unsurprisingly, for exploring love as ecstatic union. In 'The Sunne Rising' the sun annoyingly shines 'Through windowes, and through curtaines' to wake the lovers, but in 'The Good-Morrow' they wake and blissfully look into each other's eyes, their love making 'one little roome, an every where'. The perfection of mutual love thus becomes rooted in a very real concrete world, which makes it much more convincing than a mere abstract statement would.

Equally unsurprisingly, the bed is the obvious setting for sexual activity or anticipation, as in the erotic Elegie XIX, 'To his Mistris Going to Bed', where the man, already naked in bed, addresses the woman undressing outside it. This poem, based on Ovid's fifth Elegy, could have been a straightforward narrative or reflective poem, but Donne has typically chosen to treat it dramatically. The woman is also outside the bed in 'The Dreame', waking the man from his dream of enjoying her but refusing to enact 'the rest'. 'The Flea' is the most fully dramatic of these poems of persuasion. The couple are in bed but the woman is denying the man. At the beginning of the second stanza he tries unsuccessfully to stop her from killing the flea ('Oh stay, three lives in one flea spare') and after her dramatic action he rebukes her in the third stanza:

Cruell and sodaine, hast thou since
Purpled thy naile, in blood of innocence?

Her reply, given in reported speech — 'thou . . . saist that thou/
Find'st not thy selfe . . . the weaker', traps her into being unable
to deny the man's final argument that he can therefore enjoy her
as easily. The setting, action and dialogue combine to create a
complete dramatic scene.

The bed is not always such a blissful setting. In 'A Feaver' it
is a sickbed, but again used to explore the strength of love: 'thou
canst not die'. In some poems it is a deathbed, though this is
rarely a tragic setting. It enables the man to reel off a satirical
list of legacies 'Before I sigh my last gaspe' in 'The Will', and in
'The Legacie' to imagine the search for a heart in his dead body
but only to discover the woman's indifferent heart which 'no
man could hold'. An extension of the deathbed is the postmortem
in 'The Dampe' to find the cause of the man's death (the woman's
disdain), 'The Funerall' where the man has died wearing an
armlet of the disdainful lady's hair, and the grave itself in 'The
Relique', but here the bracelet of hair symbolises the miracle of
love.

Several poems have an outdoor setting, such as a garden
('Twicknam Garden' and possibly 'The Blossome'), a bank of
violets ('The Extasie'), a hill at Montgomery Castle (where
Herbert was born — 'The Primrose') and just outdoors in 'A
Lecture Upon the Shadow' which, unusually for Donne, has a
precise setting in time as well as place, being delivered at noon
after a three hours' walk. An equally vivid sense of situation is
found in Satyre IV where the poet goes to court and meets the
shabby informer who tries to provoke him into giving something
away in his speech. The poem is remarkably like a scene from a
play with excellent dialogue as Donne deliberately misunder-
stands the point of the questions and displays great wit in his
absurd answers.

In no less than eight poems — the four 'Valedictions', two
valedictory Elegies (V, 'His Picture', and XVI, 'On his Mistris'),
'The Expiration' and the Song 'Sweetest love, I do not goe' — the
situation is the parting of two lovers. There is no hint of
cynicism in these poems and the situation is used to explore the
idea expressed in Elegie XVI, 'On his Mistris', 'That absent

lovers one in th'other bee'. Elegie V, 'His Picture', paints the very dramatic picture of the man wondering how the woman will accept him if he returns maimed from his sea voyage 'My body'a sack of bones, broken within'.

It is worth comparing the Elegie 'On his Mistris' with its extravagant conceits of mutual love (and those of the 'Valedictions' and many others) with actual drama of the London stage of the 1590s. Consider the drama of these lines near the end of the Elegie:

> nor in bed fright thy nurse
> With midnights startings, crying out, oh, oh,
> Nurse, oh my love is slaine; I saw him goe,
> Ore the white Alpes, alone; I saw him, I,
> Assayld, fight, taken, stabb'd, bleede, fall, and dye.

Both in dramatic concept, impact, and the actual use of language this is remarkably similar to lines from Shakespeare's *Romeo and Juliet*:

> JULIET   'Romeo is banishèd!' to speak that word
>   Is father, mother, Tybalt, Romeo, Juliet,
>   All slain, all dead: 'Romeo is banishèd!'
>   There is no end, limit, measure, bound
>   In that word's death; no words can that woe sound.

> (III.2.122–126)

> NURSE   O! she says nothing, sir, but weeps and weeps;
>   And now falls on her bed; and then starts up,
>   And Tybalt calls, and then on Romeo cries,
>   And then falls down again.

> (III.3.98–101)

The use of patterning and repetition is striking; for example Shakespeare has four nouns in one line and Donne has a line consisting, apart from the word 'and', entirely of no less than seven verbs. His poetry is full of the extravagance typical of Elizabethan drama; for example in 'The Will':

> But I'll undoe
> The world by dying; because love dies too.

Surely Donne would have been a very successful dramatist had he chosen to write for the stage.

His use of forceful explosive language is most striking in the openings of many poems. Many begin with an imperative verb, or contain an imperative in the first few words, dramatically grabbing the reader's attention:

Goe and catch a falling starre   ('Song')

Come, Madam, come   (Elegie XIX, 'To his Mistris Going to Bed')

Spit in my face you Jewes, and pierce my side   (Holy Sonnet XI)

Batter my heart, three person'd God   (Holy Sonnet XIV)

Show me deare Christ, thy Spouse   (Holy Sonnet XVIII)

For Godsake hold your tongue, and let me love ('The Canonization')

So, so, breake off this last lamenting kisse   ('The Expiration')

Oh doe not die   ('A Feaver')

Having started with a bang, some poems continue or end with a string of imperatives, such as the direct appeal to Christ in 'Good Friday, 1613: Riding Westwards':

O thinke mee worth thine anger, punish mee,
Burne off my rusts, and my deformity

It is indeed in the religious poems that dramatic language is used with the most daring audacity, most notably in Holy Sonnet XIV, 'Batter my heart, three person'd God; for, you', which cries out to God in a powerful rhythmic sequence of alliterative monosyllables: 'bend/ Your force, to breake, blowe, burn and make me new' and ends with the amazing appeal:

Divorce mee, 'untie, or breake that knot againe,
Take mee to you, imprison mee, for I
Except you'enthrall mee, never shall be free,
Nor ever chast, except you ravish mee.

This degree of passionate intensity is also seen sometimes in the religious poetry of George Herbert, and I would argue that Herbert, who was strongly influenced by Donne, is the next most dramatic of all the metaphysical poets. A similarity is immediately apparent if we look at the opening lines of some of

Herbert's poems and compare them with the first lines of Donne quoted above:

> Ah my deare angrie Lord,
> Since thou dost love, yet strike   ('Bitter-Sweet')

> Sorrie I am, my God, sorrie I am   ('Sinnes Round')

> Come my Way my Truth my Life   ('The Call')

> Alas poore Death, where is thy glorie?   ('Dialogue-Anthem')

(The last of these is remarkably like Donne's Holy Sonnet 'Death be not proud'.)

Any similarity may seem surprising when we consider that although Herbert was born only about twenty years later than Donne, in 1593, he wrote virtually all his poetry in the last four years of his life (1630–33) while vicar of the tiny rural backwater of Bemerton, where he had retired after failing to gain the glittering prizes of state office he had once expected. But the difficulty of reconciling himself to this apparent failure in worldly terms and accepting a very different spiritual purpose for his life became the subject of many poems. The subject is essentially conflict, and, as is frequently stated, conflict is the very essence of drama.

Herbert's treatment of this conflict is seen at its most dramatic in 'The Collar', which begins with the priest suddenly rebelling with extreme violence against God's service:

> I struck the board, and cry'd, No more.
> I will abroad.

The near-blasphemous shock of this opening is surely as dramatic as anything in Donne, containing not only forceful language, but an explicit location with a character using direct speech. Admittedly the character is Herbert himself but he has given himself a persona of ill-mannered rudeness who 'rav'd and grew more fierce and wilde'. The poem ends quietly but still dramatically with the sudden voice of God calling 'Child', and Herbert's moving reply of submission: 'My Lord'. This pattern of a shock opening and a gentle ending is different from Donne, and is seen in a number of poems, such as 'The Crosse', where we hear the voice of the malcontent suffering both physical and spiritual illness and muttering seditiously against the injustice of God in taking away 'my power to serve thee'. The poem concludes again with the rebellion under control in the quiet but very firm words 'Thy will be done'. In 'The Flower', which is like a sequel to 'The Crosse', we hear a different voice, rejecting the self-centred pride of the rebel and affirming with conviction the splendour of a new life in the wonder of God's love:

> And now in age I bud again

This mastery of the subtle nuances of the spoken voice and of colloquial dialogue is one of the most remarkable features of Herbert's poetry, and it is of course essentially a feature of drama. The range is considerable, from the everyday naturalness of:

> Who would have thought my shrivel'd heart
> Could have recover'd greennesse?
>
> ('The Flower')

and the courteous good manners of the host in 'Love':

> You must sit downe . . . and taste my meat

to the emotional cry which interrupts God's voice as the final line of 'Dialogue':

> Ah! no more: thou break'st my heart.

The drama of many of Herbert's poems is indeed heightened by his use of dialogue, which Donne uses only sparingly. The voices are frequently those of Herbert himself and God, as in 'Dialogue', and a common technique is to bring the poem to a decisive end with a different voice, as here or in 'Redemption', which concludes with the matter-of-fact voice of God — 'Your suit is granted'.

There are variations on the Herbert–God dialogue, such as that between Christian and Death in 'Dialogue–Anthem', or the playfully witty replies of Echo in 'Heaven' which cleverly repeat the last part of the previous word, or the intriguing and distracting voices in 'The Quip' of Beautie, Money, Glorie, Wit and Conversation, some of them allowed direct speech and some suggested indirectly, with Herbert relying on God to answer them for him by simply saying 'I am thine'.

Herbert makes less use than Donne of dramatic action, but several poems do use it effectively, for example 'Love' with its invitation to sit at the table for a meal, or 'Redemption' where the tenant seeks his lord first in heaven then on earth, eventually finding him as Christ at the very moment of his death on the cross — as daring in its dramatic conception as any of Donne's poems.

The effect of all these dramatic techniques which I have explored in the poetry of Donne and Herbert is that as readers we are cast in the role of the audience, and as in the theatre we participate in the drama by responding to the voices, and becoming caught up in the action or situation. We are in a real sense *involved*, and this involvement of the audience is at the heart of all dramatic experience.

AFTERTHOUGHTS

1

Why do you think Lewis suggests that writing for the stage would have been 'beneath [Donne's] dignity' (page 98)?

2

Why should we assume that Donne speaks in his 'own' voice (page 102) in his religious poetry, but not in his secular poetry?

3

Do you agree that the couple described in 'The Flea' are necessarily in bed at the beginning of that poem (page 102)?

4

How else might a reader become '*involved*' (page 108) with a poem, other than by the means noted in this essay?

Nigel Smith

Nigel Smith is Fellow and Tutor in English Literature at Keble College, Oxford. He is the author of numerous critical works.

ESSAY

The metaphysical Penguin

Most of us come to that group of early and mid-seventeenth-century poets known as the 'metaphysicals' by way of the Penguin anthology entitled *The Metaphysical Poets*, assembled by Helen Gardner and first published in 1957 (revised 1966 and 1972). It is frequently set in A-level syllabuses, and is also often used in degree courses. Indeed, with the exception of Shakespeare texts, it has, since its appearance, probably been the most important vehicle for the popularising of English Renaissance verse in the world, certainly in Britain. The edition is notable for the selection of poetry offered (a good deal of Donne, Herbert, Marvell and Vaughan). But it is also well known for its brief and judicious introductory essay. Here, generations of students have learnt to define 'metaphysical': Helen Gardner explains that it was originally applied to Donne and his friends as a term of disdain and some disapproval by later poets (principally Dryden and Johnson), who thought that such poetry was too clever-clever by far, and that its inventiveness and obscurity were unnatural, especially for verse which was often concerned with the simple pleasures of (erotic) love. Those students who persevered with Helen Gardner's Introduction will also have learnt that this ingeniousness is manifested in two features — first, the 'conceit', where a 'witty' comparison is made so that our attention focuses more on the nature of the comparison than the subject-matter itself; and second, the development of the so-called 'strong line', of a poetry distinctly unornamental, employing plain vocabulary and the rhythms of conversation.

When Helen Gardner wrote the first version of her Introduction, she was in a sense still attempting to rescue the 'metaphysicals' from the oblivion into which they had been cast by eighteenth- and nineteenth-century poets and critics. The credit of resurrecting the 'metaphysicals' falls to the scholar Sir Herbert Grierson (in his own anthology and in his important 1912 edition of Donne), and T S Eliot. Donne, along with some of the Jacobean dramatists (especially Webster) were lined up by Eliot in a new tradition of literary greatness (ending in Eliot himself) in which — he argues — poetry is to be valued for its ability to register the painfulness and immediacy of real experience, without the detractions of florid verse conventions or imitations of the classics. Donne was especially important for Eliot because in Donne's verse thought was feeling and feeling was thought, thus displaying a 'unified sensibility' which the rise of modern science and dominant middle-class literary forms (the novel) quickly removed by the end of the seventeenth century. So in 1957, when Eliot was still alive and very much a force in English letters, Helen Gardner was turning the viewpoint of an influential modernist writer into an orthodoxy which has remained with us ever since.

What is wrong with Helen Gardner's Introduction, and why should we be concerned with it? It is after all a masterpiece of tact and concision, and since it has been so influential, to argue with it is like trying to deny the existence of historical facts. What we think about it depends very much on how we choose to value poetry. The Victorians valued long narrative verse with regular forms, sometimes as song, and had little time for what they considered ugly over-wrought introspection (though Herbert's verse would be an exception here). The Romantics and the Victorians valued to a large extent poetry which was politically engaged, and which embodied a conception of liberty in its very form and operation, such as the poet Edmund Spenser's epic of Elizabethan national glory *The Faerie Queene* (1590–93). 'Metaphysical' verse is seemingly not public — it deals with private, intimate matters (such as Donne's lovers in bed), or the spiritual dilemmas of the individual believer. Is the twentieth century (that which has largely gone, and that little left to come) also so resolutely introverted? Or is metaphysical poetry itself part of an educationally induced drug which blinds us to the necessity of a vibrant tradition of public verse meant to flourish in the good life of a nation?

One could ask many similar questions, and it does not take too long for attentive readers to feel very dissatisfied with the Gardner Introduction, to feel that the wool is being pulled over their eyes in a clever act of presenting a poetic 'tradition' where none in fact exists. Also, attention to the purportedly 'purely poetic' qualities of 'metaphysical' verse forecloses consideration of other issues which help us to see why 'metaphysical' poetry is as it is, and how we might have a way of viewing the poetry not as the exclusive and most valuable literary precursor of the Modern, but as a peculiar kind of response to literary and social forces at a certain moment in time.

The verse of Donne, Herbert, Marvell, Vaughan, and the rest, was on the whole not widely read in the lifetimes of its authors. Spenserean epic and allegorical verse was the popular verse-form through to the middle of the seventeenth century. People read this material more easily, and said so. Nowadays, few have the time to read long narrative accounts of virtue, and it is hard to see why these poems which appear to us so inferior in every way to the brief conceited lyric should have been so popular. But they were. What we call 'metaphysical' verse was occasional, frivolous, largely written to circulate in the restricted milieu of one's friends. It was distraction, at best produced to manifest certain skills of eloquence and wit at the point of one's initiation into manhood, before one progressed to weightier matters, like affairs of state.

A proof of this is that very little 'metaphysical' verse was published during the authors' lifetimes. Donne, Herbert and Marvell's poetry was published in complete and collected form only after their deaths. Donne's primary reputation in his own time was as a clergyman (James I appointed him Dean of St Paul's Cathedral in 1621). Ten years after his death, the work which counted most for his reputation was the folio edition of his sermons of 1640. When Marvell at last found himself in the public employ (first as a Cromwellian civil servant, then as a Restoration Member of Parliament), he very largely ceased to write (as far as we know) any lyric verse. In any case, his 'An *Horatian* Ode upon *Cromwel's* Return from *Ireland*' (June 1650), a poem he wrote perhaps to gain favour, is hardly 'metaphysical'. For all its brilliance, it is first and foremost an imitation of a form in which the Roman poet Horace excelled; its conceits are minimal and appropriate rather than arresting, and one wonders why Helen Gardner included it, except that it is so very good. Vaughan wrote his best poetry in retirement during the Civil War, devoid of duty and assent. He did publish his verse, but then it was performing a rather different function from the one characteristically associated with it, as we shall see.

When we turn to the more minor verse in the selection, it is also hard to see why some of it has been included as 'metaphysical'. Sir John Suckling's Sonnet 'Of thee (kind boy) I ask no red and white' is a delicate, impassioned and sensuous address to Cupid which is conventional rather than experimental in its presentation. Indeed, it clearly has more to do with Donne's predecessor Sir Philip Sidney than with Donne himself. Gardner's decision to start with the very late sixteenth century obscures the continuities with the high Elizabethan Renaissance. Sidney's verse itself is conceited: 'Alas, if this the only metall be/ Of *Love*, new-coind to helpe my beggary,/ Deare, love me not, that you may love me more.' Donne and Suckling appear in this light more attractive and more various. Their verse has the potential to sustain our attention in our awareness of a greater diversity. In his poem 'Jordan (I)', George Herbert (who was distantly related to Sidney, although Sidney died before Herbert was born) can be seen revising the traditions of courtly pastoral verse by which Sidney expressed his personal and political ambitions: 'Who sayes that fictions onely and false hair/ Become a verse? Is there in truth no beautie?/ ... Is it no verse except enchanted groves/ And sudden arbours shadow coarse-spunne lines?' The case for a wide perspective on tradition seems overwhelming. Gardner admits that Elizabethan verse is conceited but she says that what makes the verse of the next century different is 'the use which they make of the conceit and the rigorous nature of their conceits, springing from the use to which they are put, which is more important'. It is hard to see how the cases of Suckling or Herbert presented here fit with such an assessment.

E

Gardner then proceeds: 'In a metaphysical poem the conceits are instruments of definition in an argument or instruments to persuade.' If this is so, why? Such a question leads us to probe into the social background of the 'metaphysical poets', a procedure seldom pursued seriously by critics before the current generation. Renaissance verse is the expression mostly of male courtiers, gentlemen and clerics. As such, it constitutes a series of fictions of identity, versions of 'selfhood', by which the experience of being such a person is structured as a continuous organisation of words. The legal or theological arguments used by Donne, whether fallacious or not, are a means of asserting selfhood. But of course, the very confines of poetry are a constraint on such expression. As much as the sense of the erotic is there in some of Donne's poems, so also there is the textual registering of frustration inherent in the poet's role: after all, a poet *is* a poet, not a lover. 'A Nocturnall upon S. Lucies day' has been regarded as a poem written to a patroness, perhaps Lucy, Countess of Bedford, the subject of other Donne poems. The job of a patronised poet is to praise the powerful person doing the patronising. The poem starts with the characteristically egotistical speaker, who has become less than nothing in his lover's despair. But then the poem turns around: in the fourth and fifth stanzas, the voice of the poet seems to recognise that he, as a poetic fiction, is not able to do what a healthy man should, that is, to impregnate: 'Were I a man, that I were one,/ I needs must know'. He is not an 'ordinary nothing' but far more ethereal than that, so that as the voice of a poet he cannot even cast a shadow. All he can do is to invoke fecundity ('To fetch new lust') rather than make fecundity a reality. By the end of this highly sophisticated poem, the alchemical conceit has become a way of describing not only love but the functions of (love) poetry, and at this point the speaking voice becomes far less selfish than is customary in Donne: 'let mee call/ This houre her Vigill, and her Eve'. Most people tend to think of Donne's poetry as if it were the voice of an authentic personality, but here we see how role-playing and the demands of expressive conventions create a complex textual play of forces of identity — of the power that confirms an identity, and that which takes it away.

At this point one can begin to see a concern in 'metaphysical' verse with structures and substances which link the components of the universe together, and which are therefore the sinews of identity. Alchemy was seriously entertained in the Renaissance as a description of forces which impelled the universe and mankind, not simply as a reservoir of images for witty poets. Unfortunately, the effect of Gardner's selection has been to isolate these kinds of imagery as effects, where the choice of other poems, particularly in the case of Donne's poetry, enables us to see the verse functioning as an instrument capable of exploring the physical world. In Elegie VIII, 'The Comparison', Donne's poetry interweaves the extravagant hyperbolic praise of love conventions, with their opposites, the description of the functioning body, and the body as a material commodity, no different to any other piece of earth: 'Ranke sweaty froth thy mistress' brow defiles,/ Like spermatic issue of ripe menstrous boils'. Sex becomes the furnace of alchemy and of war:

> Then like the chimick's masculine equal fire,
> Which in the limbeck's warm womb doth inspire
> Into th'earth's worthless dirt a soul of gold,
> Such cherishing heat her best loved part doth hold.
> Thine's like the dread mouth of a fired gun,
> Or like hot liquid metals newly run.

(ll.35–40)

If we view the sum total of such effects, then we do not have merely a set of conceits but a linguistic means of organising the world. It is a way of thinking which, T S Eliot believed, we have lost, but to treat it just as poetic achievement is to make it more modern and less strange than is the case. Had we but world enough, and time, we could see how such writing is a feature of other discourses, Donne's own prose or seventeenth-century medical books, for instance. Indeed, Henry Vaughan and his brother Thomas believed that alchemy and its sister discipline, occult philosophy, were a means to the health of the body as much as theology was a cure for the soul. In this light, Vaughan's poetry becomes a medicine for the total regeneration of the human soul and body:

> Father of lights! what Sunnie seed,
> What glance of day hast thou confin'd
> Into this bird? To all the breed

This busie Ray thou hast assign'd;
    Their magnetisme works all night,
    And dreams of Paradise and light.

('Cock-crowing', ll.1–6)

So, when we read the Penguin *Metaphysical Poets*, it is well worth pondering how it has been organised, what ideas have dictated the choice of poems. All anthologies are choices, and no single anthology has yet replaced Gardner. It probably never will: the next Penguin anthology in the area will be a book of 'Renaissance' verse, covering a broader time-span, and with concerns more closely attuned to the longer poetry referred to in the earlier part of this essay. All the more reason, then, to treat an anthology and its introduction as an essay itself, and to go behind it, to read the poets themselves in the most open way possible.

AFTERTHOUGHTS

1

What do you understand by 'thought was feeling and feeling was thought' (page 111)?

2

What do you understand by 'part of an educationally induced drug' (page 112)?

3

In what ways does Smith challenge the selection criteria of *The Metaphysical Poets* (page 113)?

4

What arguments does Smith put forward to suggest that what we think of as 'metaphysical' poetry comprises not merely 'a set of conceits' but 'a linguistic means of organising the world' (page 115)?

INTRODUCTION

First, a word of warning. Good essays are the product of a creative engagement with literature. So never try to restrict your studies to what you think will be 'useful in the exam'. Ironically, you will restrict your grade potential if you do.

This doesn't mean, of course, that you should ignore the basic skills of essay writing. When you read critics, make a conscious effort to notice *how* they communicate their ideas. The guidelines that follow offer advice of a more explicit kind. But they are no substitute for practical experience. It is never easy to express ideas with clarity and precision. But the more often you tackle the problems involved and experiment to find your own voice, the more fluent you will become. So practise writing essays as often as possible.

HOW TO PLAN
AN ESSAY

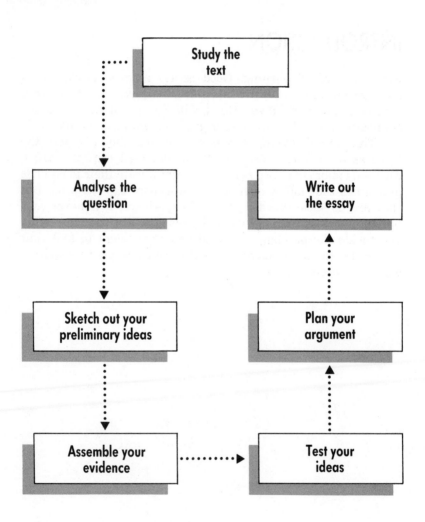

Study the text

The first step in writing a good essay is to get to know the set text well. Never write about a text until you are fully familiar with it. Even a discussion of the opening chapter of a novel, for example, should be informed by an understanding of the book as a whole. Literary texts, however, are by their very nature complex and on a first reading you are bound to miss many significant features. Re-read the book with care, if possible more than once. Look up any unfamiliar words in a good dictionary and if the text you are studying was written more than a few decades ago, consult the *Oxford English Dictionary* to find out whether the meanings of any terms have shifted in the intervening period.

Good books are difficult to put down when you first read them. But a more leisurely second or third reading gives you the opportunity to make notes on those features you find significant. An index of characters and events is often useful, particularly when studying novels with a complex plot or time scheme. The main aim, however, should be to record your *responses* to the text. By all means note, for example, striking images. But be sure to add *why* you think them striking. Similarly, record any thoughts you may have on interesting comparisons with other texts, puzzling points of characterisation, even what you take to be aesthetic blemishes. The important thing is to annotate fully and adventurously. The most seemingly idiosyncratic comment may later lead to a crucial area of discussion which you would otherwise have overlooked. It helps to have a working copy of the text in which to mark up key passages and jot down marginal comments (although obviously these practices are taboo when working with library, borrowed or valuable copies!). But keep a fuller set of notes as well and organise these under appropriate headings.

Literature does not exist in an aesthetic vacuum, however, and you should try to find out as much as possible about the context of its production and reception. It is particularly important to read other works by the same author and writings by contemporaries. At this early stage, you may want to restrict your secondary reading to those standard reference works, such as biographies, which are widely available in public libraries. In the long run, however, it pays to read as wide a range of critical studies as possible.

Some students, and tutors, worry that such studies may stifle the development of any truly personal response. But this won't happen if you are alert to the danger and read critically. After all, you wouldn't passively accept what a stranger told you in conversation. The fact that a critic's views are in print does not necessarily make them any more authoritative (as a glance at the review pages of the *TLS* and *London Review of Books* will reveal). So question the views you find: 'Does this critic's interpretation agree with mine and where do we part company?' 'Can it be right to try and restrict this text's meanings to those found by its author or first audience?' 'Doesn't this passage treat a theatrical text as though it were a novel?' Often it is views which you reject which prove most valuable since they challenge you to articulate your own position with greater clarity. Be sure to keep careful notes on what the critic wrote, and your *reactions* to what the critic wrote.

Analyse the question

You cannot begin to answer a question until you understand what task it is you have been asked to perform. Re-cast the question in your own words and reconstruct the line of reasoning which lies behind it. Where there is a choice of topics, try to choose the one for which you are best prepared. It would, for example, be unwise to tackle 'How far do you agree that in *Paradise Lost* Milton transformed the epic models he inherited from ancient Greece and Rome?' without a working knowledge of Homer and Virgil (or *Paradise Lost* for that matter!). If you do not already know the works of these authors, the question should spur you on to read more widely — or discourage you from attempting it at all. The scope of an essay, however, is not always so obvious and you must remain alert to the implied demands of each question. How could you possibly 'Consider the view that *Wuthering Heights* transcends the conventions of the Gothic novel' without reference to at least some of those works which, the question suggests, have *not* transcended Gothic conventions?

When you have decided on a topic, analyse the terms of the question itself. Sometimes these self-evidently require careful definition: *tragedy* and *irony*, for example, are notoriously difficult concepts to pin down and you will probably need to consult a good dictionary of literary terms. Don't ignore, however, those seemingly innocuous phrases which often smuggle in significant assumptions. 'Does Macbeth lack the nobility of the true tragic hero?' obviously invites you to discuss nobility and the nature of the tragic hero. But what of 'lack' and 'true' — do they suggest that the play would be improved had Shakespeare depicted Macbeth in a different manner? or that tragedy is superior to other forms of drama? Remember that you are not expected meekly to agree with the assumptions implicit in the question. Some questions are deliberately provocative in order to stimulate an engaged response. Don't be afraid to take up the challenge.

Sketch out your preliminary ideas

'Which comes first, the evidence or the answer?' is one of those chicken and egg questions. How can you form a view without inspecting the evidence? But how can you know which evidence is relevant without some idea of what it is you are looking for? In practice the mind reviews evidence and formulates preliminary theories or hypotheses at one and the same time, although for the sake of clarity we have separated out the processes. Remember that these early ideas are only there to get you started. You *expect* to modify them in the light of the evidence you uncover. Your initial hypothesis may be an instinctive 'gut-reaction'. Or you may find that you prefer to 'sleep on the problem', allowing ideas to gell over a period of time. Don't worry in either case. The mind is quite capable of processing a vast amount of accumulated evidence, the product of previous reading and thought, and reaching sophisticated intuitive judgements. Eventually, however, you are going to have to think carefully through any ideas you arrive at by such intuitive processes. Are they logical? Do they take account of all the relevant factors? Do they fully answer the question set? Are there any obvious reasons to qualify or abandon them?

Assemble your evidence

Now is the time to return to the text and re-read it with the question and your working hypothesis firmly in mind. Many of the notes you have already made are likely to be useful, but assess the precise relevance of this material and make notes on any new evidence you discover. The important thing is to cast your net widely and take into account points which tend to undermine your case as well as those that support it. As always, ensure that your notes are full, accurate, and reflect your own critical judgements.

You may well need to go outside the text if you are to do full justice to the question. If you think that the 'Oedipus complex' may be relevant to an answer on *Hamlet* then read Freud and a balanced selection of those critics who have discussed the appropriateness of applying psychoanalytical theories to the interpretation of literature. Their views can most easily be tracked down by consulting the annotated bibliographies held by most major libraries (and don't be afraid to ask a librarian for help in finding and using these). Remember that you go to works of criticism not only to obtain information but to stimulate you into clarifying your own position. And that since life is short and many critical studies are long, judicious use of a book's index and/or contents list is not to be scorned. You can save yourself a great deal of future labour if you carefully record full bibliographic details at this stage.

Once you have collected the evidence, organise it coherently. Sort the detailed points into related groups and identify the quotations which support these. You must also assess the relative importance of each point, for in an essay of limited length it is essential to establish a firm set of priorities, exploring some ideas in depth while discarding or subordinating others.

Test your ideas

As we stressed earlier, a hypothesis is only a proposal, and one that you fully expect to modify. Review it with the evidence before you. Do you really still believe in it? It would be surprising if you did not want to modify it in some way. If you cannot see any problems, others may. Try discussing your ideas with friends and relatives. Raise them in class discussions. Your tutor is certain to welcome your initiative. The critical process is essentially collaborative and there is absolutely no reason why you should not listen to and benefit from the views of others. Similarly, you should feel free to test your ideas against the theories put forward in academic journals and books. But do not just borrow what you find. Critically analyse the views on offer and, where appropriate, integrate them into your own pattern of thought. You must, of course, give full acknowledgement to the sources of such views.

Do not despair if you find you have to abandon or modify significantly your initial position. The fact that you are prepared to do so is a mark of intellectual integrity. Dogmatism is never an academic virtue and many of the best essays explore the *process* of scholarly enquiry rather than simply record its results.

Plan your argument

Once you have more or less decided on your attitude to the question (for an answer is never really 'finalised') you have to present your case in the most persuasive manner. In order to do this you must avoid meandering from point to point and instead produce an organised argument — a structured flow of ideas and supporting evidence, leading logically to a conclusion which fully answers the question. Never begin to write until you have produced an outline of your argument.

You may find it easiest to begin by sketching out its main stages as a flow chart or some other form of visual presentation. But eventually you should produce a list of paragraph topics. The paragraph is the conventional written demarcation for a unit of thought and you can outline an argument quite simply by briefly summarising the substance of each paragraph and then checking that these points (you may remember your English teacher referring to them as topic sentences) really do follow a coherent order. Later you will be able to elaborate on each topic, illustrating and qualifying it as you go along. But you will find this far easier to do if you possess from the outset a clear map of where you are heading.

All questions require some form of an argument. Even so-called 'descriptive' questions *imply* the need for an argument. An adequate answer to the request to 'Outline the role of Iago in *Othello*' would do far more than simply list his appearances on stage. It would at the very least attempt to provide some *explanation* for his actions — is he, for example, a representative stage 'Machiavel'? an example of pure evil, 'motiveless malignity'? or a realistic study of a tormented personality reacting to identifiable social and psychological pressures?

Your conclusion ought to address the terms of the question. It may seem obvious, but 'how far do you agree', 'evaluate', 'consider', 'discuss', etc, are *not* interchangeable formulas and your conclusion must take account of the precise wording of the question. If asked 'How far do you agree?', the concluding paragraph of your essay really should state whether you are in complete agreement, total disagreement, or, more likely, partial agreement. Each preceding paragraph should have a clear justification for its existence and help to clarify the reasoning which underlies your conclusion. If you find that a paragraph serves no good purpose (perhaps merely summarising the plot), do not hesitate to discard it.

The arrangement of the paragraphs, the overall strategy of the argument, can vary. One possible pattern is dialectical: present the arguments in favour of one point of view (**thesis**); then turn to counter-arguments or to a rival interpretation (**antithesis**); finally evaluate the competing claims and arrive at your own conclusion (**synthesis**). You may, on the other hand, feel so convinced of the merits of one particular case that you wish to devote your entire essay to arguing that viewpoint persuasively (although it is always desirable to indicate, however briefly, that you are aware of alternative, if flawed, positions). As the essays contained in this volume demonstrate, there are many other possible strategies. Try to adopt the one which will most comfortably accommodate the demands of the question and allow you to express your thoughts with the greatest possible clarity.

Be careful, however, not to apply abstract formulas in a mechanical manner. It is true that you should be careful to define your terms. It is *not* true that every essay should begin with 'The dictionary defines x as . . .'. In fact, definitions are often best left until an appropriate moment for their introduction arrives. Similarly every essay should have a beginning, middle and end. But it does not follow that in your opening paragraph you should announce an intention to write an essay, or that in your concluding paragraph you need to signal an imminent desire to put down your pen. The old adages are often useful reminders of what constitutes good practice, but they must be interpreted intelligently.

Write out the essay

Once you have developed a coherent argument you should aim to communicate it in the most effective manner possible. Make certain you clearly identify yourself, and the question you are answering. Ideally, type your answer, or at least ensure your handwriting is legible and that you leave sufficient space for your tutor's comments. Careless presentation merely distracts from the force of your argument. Errors of grammar, syntax and spelling are far more serious. At best they are an irritating blemish, particularly in the work of a student who should be sensitive to the nuances of language. At worst, they seriously confuse the sense of your argument. If you are aware that you have stylistic problems of this kind, ask your tutor for advice at the earliest opportunity. Everyone, however, is liable to commit the occasional howler. The only remedy is to give yourself plenty of time in which to proof-read your manuscript (often reading it aloud is helpful) before submitting it.

Language, however, is not only an instrument of communication; it is also an instrument of thought. If you want to think clearly and precisely you should strive for a clear, precise prose style. Keep your sentences short and direct. Use modern, straightforward English wherever possible. Avoid repetition, clichés and wordiness. Beware of generalisations, simplifications, and overstatements. Orwell analysed the relationship between stylistic vice and muddled thought in his essay 'Politics and the English Language' (1946) — it remains essential reading (and is still readily available in volume 4 of the Penguin *Collected Essays, Journalism and Letters*). Generalisations, for example, are always dangerous. They are rarely true and tend to suppress the individuality of the texts in question. A remark such as 'Keats always employs sensuous language in his poetry' is not only fatuous (what, after all, does it mean? is *every* word he wrote equally 'sensuous'?) but tends to obscure interesting distinctions which could otherwise be made between, say, the descriptions in the 'Ode on a Grecian Urn' and those in 'To Autumn'.

The intelligent use of quotations can help you make your points with greater clarity. Don't sprinkle them throughout your essay without good reason. There is no need, for example, to use them to support uncontentious statements of fact. 'Macbeth murdered Duncan' does not require textual evidence (unless you wish to dispute Thurber's brilliant parody, 'The Macbeth Murder Mystery', which reveals Lady Macbeth's father as the culprit!). Quotations should be included, however, when they are necessary to support your case. The proposition that Macbeth's imaginative powers wither after he has killed his king would certainly require extensive quotation: you would almost certainly want to analyse key passages from both before and after the murder (perhaps his first and last soliloquies?). The key word here is 'analyse'. Quotations cannot make your points on their own. It is up to you to demonstrate their relevance and clearly explain to your readers *why* you want them to focus on the passage you have selected.

Most of the academic conventions which govern the presentation of essays are set out briefly in the style sheet below. The question of gender, however, requires fuller discussion. More than half the population of the world is female. Yet many writers still refer to an undifferentiated *man*kind. Or write of the author and *his* public. We do not think that this convention has much to recommend it. At the very least, it runs the risk of introducing unintended sexist attitudes. And at times leads to such patent absurdities as 'Cleopatra's final speech asserts *man*'s true nobility'. With a little thought, you can normally find ways of expressing yourself which do not suggest that the typical author, critic or reader is male. Often you can simply use plural forms, which is probably a more elegant solution than relying on such awkward formulations as 's/he' or 'he and she'. You should also try to avoid distinguishing between male and female authors on the basis of forenames. Why *Jane* Austen and not *George* Byron? Refer to all authors by their last names unless there is some good reason not to. Where there may otherwise be confusion, say between T S and George Eliot, give the name in full when if first occurs and thereafter use the last name only.

Finally, keep your audience firmly in mind. Tutors and examiners are interested in understanding your conclusions and the processes by which you arrived at them. They are not interested in reading a potted version of a book they already know. **So don't pad out your work with plot summary.**

Hints for examinations

In an examination you should go through exactly the same processes as you would for the preparation of a term essay. The only difference lies in the fact that some of the stages will have had to take place before you enter the examination room. This should not bother you unduly. Examiners are bound to avoid the merely eccentric when they come to formulate papers and if you have read widely and thought deeply about the central issues raised by your set texts you can be confident you will have sufficient material to answer the majority of questions sensibly.

The fact that examinations impose strict time limits makes it *more* rather than less, important that you plan carefully. There really is no point in floundering into an answer without any idea of where you are going, particularly when there will not be time to recover from the initial error.

Before you begin to answer any question at all, study the entire paper with care. Check that you understand the rubric and know how many questions you have to answer and whether any are compulsory. It may be comforting to spot a title you feel confident of answering well, but don't rush to tackle it: read *all* the questions before deciding which *combination* will allow you to display your abilities to the fullest advantage. Once you have made your choice, analyse each question, sketch out your ideas, assemble the evidence, review your initial hypothesis, plan your argument, *before* trying to write out an answer. And make notes at each stage: not only will these help you arrive at a sensible conclusion, but examiners are impressed by evidence of careful thought.

Plan your time as well as your answers. If you have practised writing timed essays as part of your revision, you should not find this too difficult. There can be a temptation to allocate extra time to the questions you know you can answer well; but this is always a short-sighted policy. You will find yourself left to face a question which would in any event have given you difficulty without even the time to give it serious thought. It is, moreover, easier to gain marks at the lower end of the scale than at the upper, and you will never compensate for one poor answer by further polishing two satisfactory answers. Try to leave some time at the end of the examination to re-read your answers and correct any obvious errors. If the worst comes to the worst and you run short of time, don't just keep writing until you are forced to break off in mid-paragraph. It is far better to provide for the examiner a set of notes which indicate the overall direction of your argument.

Good luck — but if you prepare for the examination conscientiously and tackle the paper in a methodical manner, you won't need it!

a minor Metaphysical poet, he relishes quaint and dotty [...] in 'Upon Appleton House', for instance, the local fish[...]

> ... like Antipodes in shoes,
> Have shod their heads in their canoes;
> How tortoise-like, but not so slow,
> These rational amphibii go!⁷

[...]her times, as in satires li[k]e 'The Last Ins[...] [...], he anticipates the Augustan urbanity (a[...] [...] couplets) of a mature [D]ryden or an Alex[...] [...]e satirises the Countess o[f] Castlemaine, a m[...] [...]harles II:

> Paint *Castlemaine* in colours that [w]ill hold
> (Her, not her picture, for she now gr[o]ws old):
> She through her lackey's drawers, as [h]e ran,
> Discerned love's cause, and a new flame [b]egan
>
> . . .
>
> Poring within her glass she re-adjusts
> Her looks, and oft-tried beauty now distrusts;
> Fears lest he scorn a woman once assayed,
> And now first wished she e'er had been a maid.
> Great Love, how dost thou triumph and how reign,
> That to a groom couldst humble her disdain!⁸

At his finest, though, in 'The Garden' and 'To His Coy Mistress', that Augustan poise in tone blends with, and controls, the mental shock-tactics of the ·conceit; and Marvell's distinctively sensuous, colourful imagining of location and situation converts what might have been merely quaint into the richly fantastic or surrealistic. Here, in 'The Garden', he offers benign transformations, firstly of the Ovidian legends in which deities sought to rape mortals, and secondly of the biblical account of the Fall of man:

> *Apollo* hunted *Daphne* so,
> Only that She might Laurel grow.

---

7 *Andrew Marvell: The Complete Poems*, ed. E S Donno (Harmondsworth, 1972), p. 99.
8 *Andrew Marvell: The Complete Poems*, p. [1]59.

Annotations (handwritten callouts):

- long verse quotations, indented and introduced by a colon. Quotation marks are not needed. The poem from which a quotation is taken should be given in brackets at the end of the quotation or (as here) specified in the surrounding text.
- Three dots (ellipsis) indicate where words or phrases have been cut from a quotation or where (as in the first example) a quotation begins mid-sentence.
- poem titles in quotation marks.
- indication of footnote
- footnotes supplying bibliographical information as specified on pages 134 - 135.
- Book/poetry collection titles in italics. In a handwritten or typed manuscript this would appear as underlining: <u>Andrew Marvell: The Complete Poem</u>.

We have divided the following information into two sections. Part A describes those rules which it is essential to master no matter what kind of essay you are writing (including examination answers). Part B sets out some of the more detailed conventions which govern the documentation of essays.

PART A: LAYOUT

Titles of texts

Titles of published books, plays (of any length), long poems, pamphlets and periodicals (including newspapers and magazines), works of classical literature, and films should be underlined: e.g. <u>David Copperfield</u> (novel), <u>Twelfth Night</u> (play), <u>Paradise Lost</u> (long poem), <u>Critical Quarterly</u> (periodical), Horace's <u>Ars Poetica</u> (Classical work), <u>Apocalypse Now</u> (film).

Notice how important it is to distinguish between titles and other names. <u>Hamlet</u> is the play; Hamlet the prince. <u>Wuthering Heights</u> is the novel; Wuthering Heights the house. Underlining is the equivalent in handwritten or typed manuscripts of printed italics. So what normally appears in this volume as *Othello* would be written as <u>Othello</u> in your essay.

Titles of articles, essays, short stories, short poems, songs, chapters of books, speeches, and newspaper articles are enclosed in quotation marks; e.g. 'The Flea' (short poem), 'The Prussian Officer' (short story), 'Middleton's Chess Strategies' (article), 'Thatcher Defects!' (newspaper headline).

Exceptions: Underlining titles or placing them within quotation marks does not apply to sacred writings (e.g. Bible, Koran, Old Testament, Gospels) or parts of a book (e.g. Preface, Introduction, Appendix).

It is generally incorrect to place quotation marks around a title of a published book which you have underlined. The exception is 'titles within titles', e.g. <u>'Vanity Fair': A Critical Study</u> (title of a book about *Vanity Fair*).

Quotations

Short verse quotations of a single line or part of a line should be incorporated within quotation marks as part of the running text of your essay. Quotations of two or three lines of verse are treated in the same way, with line endings indicated by a slash(/). For example:

1 In Julius Caesar, Antony says of Brutus, 'This was the noblest Roman of them all'.
2 The opening of Antony's famous funeral oration, 'Friends, Romans, Countrymen, lend me your ears;/ I come to bury Caesar not to praise him', is a carefully controlled piece of rhetoric.

Longer verse quotations of more than three lines should be indented from the main body of the text and introduced in most cases with a colon. Do not enclose indented quotations within quotation marks. For example:

It is worth pausing to consider the reasons Brutus gives to justify his decision to assassinate Caesar:

> It must be by his death; and for my part,
> I know no personal cause to spurn at him,
> But for the general. He would be crowned.
> How might that change his nature, there's the question.

At first glance his rationale may appear logical . . .

Prose quotations of less than three lines should be incorporated in the text of the essay, within quotation marks. Longer prose quotations should be indented and the quotation marks omitted. For example:

1 Before his downfall, Caesar rules with an iron hand. His political opponents, the Tribunes Marullus and Flavius, are 'put to silence' for the trivial offence of 'pulling scarfs off Caesar's image'.
2 It is interesting to note the rhetorical structure of Brutus's Forum speech:

> Romans, countrymen, and lovers, hear me for my cause, and be silent that you may hear. Believe me for my honour, and have respect to mine honour that you may believe. Censure me in your wisdom, and awake your senses, that you may the better judge.

Tenses: When you are relating the events that occur within a work of fiction or describing the author's technique, it is the convention to use the present tense. Even though Orwell published *Animal Farm* in 1945, the book *describes* the animals' seizure of Manor Farm. Similarly, Macbeth always *murders* Duncan, despite the passage of time.

PART B: DOCUMENTATION

When quoting from verse of more than twenty lines, provide line references: e.g. In 'Upon Appleton House' Marvell's mower moves 'With whistling scythe and elbow strong' (1.393).

Quotations from plays should be identified by act, scene and line references: e.g. Prospero, in Shakespeare's The Tempest, refers to Caliban as 'A devil, a born devil' (IV.1.188). (i.e. Act 4. Scene 1. Line 188).

Quotations from prose works should provide a chapter reference and, where appropriate, a page reference.

Bibliographies should list full details of all sources consulted. The way in which they are presented varies, but one standard format is as follows:

1   Books and articles are listed in alphabetical order by the author's last name. Initials are placed after the surname.
2   If you are referring to a chapter or article within a larger work, you list it by reference to the author of the article or chapter, not the editor (although the editor is also named in the reference).
3   Give (in parentheses) the place and date of publication, e.g. (London, 1962). These details can be found within the book itself. Here are some examples:

> Brockbank, J.P., 'Shakespeare's Histories, English and Roman', in Ricks, C. (ed.) English Drama to 1710 (Sphere History of Literature in the English Language) (London, 1971).
> Gurr, A., 'Richard III and the Democratic Process', Essays in Criticism 24 (1974), pp. 39–47.
> Spivack, B., Shakespeare and the Allegory of Evil (New York, 1958).

Footnotes: In general, try to avoid using footnotes and build your references into the body of the essay wherever possible. When you do use them give the full bibliographic reference to a work in the first instance and then use a short title: e.g. See K. Smidt, Unconformities in Shakespeare's History Plays (London, 1982), pp. 43–47 becomes Smidt (pp. 43–47) thereafter. Do not use terms such as 'ibid.' or 'op. cit.' unless you are absolutely sure of their meaning.

There is a principle behind all this seeming pedantry. The reader ought to be able to find and check your references and quotations as quickly and easily as possible. Give additional information, such as canto or volume number whenever you think it will assist your reader.

SUGGESTIONS FOR FURTHER READING

Texts

Quotations from this volume are generally taken from Helen Gardner's edition of *The Metaphysical Poets* (Harmondsworth, 1961, revised 1972). Another widely influential selection, *Metaphysical Lyrics and Poems* (London, 1921) was edited by H J C Grierson.

The standard complete texts of the major metaphysical poets are

John Donne:
Divine Poems, ed. H Gardner (Oxford, 1952)
Elegies and Songs and Sonnets, ed. H Gardner (Oxford, 1965)
Sermons, ed. G R Potter and E M Simpson (Oxford, 1962)

George Herbert:
Works, ed. F E Hutchinson (Oxford, 1941)

Andrew Marvell:
Poems and Letters, ed. H M Margoliouth (Oxford, third edition, revised by P Legouis and E E Duncan-Jones, 1971)

Thomas Traherne:
Centuries, Poems and Thanksgivings, ed. H M Margoliouth (Oxford, 1958)

Henry Vaughan:
Works, ed. L C Martin (Oxford, 1957)

Students should consult *Minor Poets of the Caroline Period*, edited by G Saintsbury (Oxford, 1921) for works by other authors included in Helen Gardner's selection.

General studies

There are innumerable studies of the individual authors, particularly Donne, Herbert and Marvell, available in specialist libraries and bookshops. We list below studies of a more general nature which are widely available.

Beer, P, *Introduction to the Metaphysical Poets* (Basingstoke, 1972)

Bennett, J, *Five Metaphysical Poets* (Cambridge, 1964)

Eliot, T S, 'The Metaphysical Poets', in *Selected Essays 1917–1932* (London, 1960)

Ford, B, *From Donne To Marvell*, The Pelican Guide to English Literature, vol. 3 (Harmondsworth, 1982)

Hammond, G, *The Metaphysical Poets* (Macmillan Casebook, Basingstoke, 1974)

Keast, W R (ed.), *Seventeenth-Century English Poetry* (London, 1967)

Palmer, D J and Bradbury, M (eds.), *Metaphysical Poetry*, Stratford-upon-Avon Studies 11 (London, 1970)

Longman Group UK Limited
Longman House, Burnt Mill, Harlow, Essex, CM20 2JE, England
and Associated Companies throughout the World.

First published 1990
ISBN 0 582 06048 6

Set in 10/12pt Century Schoolbook, Linotron 202
Printed in Great Britain
by Bell and Bain Ltd., Glasgow

Acknowledgement
The editors would like to thank Zachary Leader for his assistance with
the style sheet.